Confessions of a Used Program Salesman

Confessions of a Used Program Salesman

INSTITUTIONALIZING SOFTWARE REUSE

Will Tracz

ADDISON-WESLEY PUBLISHING COMPANY

Reading, Massachusetts • Menlo Park, California • New York • Don Mills, Ontario
Wokingham, England • Amsterdam • Bonn • Paris • Milan • Madrid
Sydney • Singapore • Tokyo • Seoul • Taipei • Mexico City • San Juan

The publisher offers discounts on this book when ordered in quantity for special sales. For more information please contact:

Corporate & Professional Publishing Group
Addison-Wesley Publishing Company
One Jacob Way
Reading, Massachusetts 01867

Library of Congress Cataloging-in-Publication Data
Tracz, Will.
    Confessions of a used program salesman : institutionalizing
software reuse / Will Tracz.
      p.   cm.
    ISBN 0-201-63369-8 (acid-free paper)
    1. Computer software—Reusability.   I. Title.
QA76.76.R47T73   1995
005.1—dc20   94-25269
                                                            CIP

Text design by Wilson Graphics & Design (Kenneth J. Wilson)
Illustrations by John Wicklund

ISBN 0-201-63369-8

Text printed on recycled and acid-free paper.
1 2 3 4 5 6 7 8 9 10-CRW-98979695
First Printing, April 1995

Contents

Preface

"Before you can reuse software, there needs to be software to reuse. The trouble is that too much re-useless software exists today."

THIS BOOK represents a lifelong ambition.[1] I can't help but wonder if anyone will buy it. If you are reading this then I guess you did, or else you may be thumbing through it at some bookstore, in which case, buy the book! Trust me! And while you're at it, I have a few nice programs in the trunk of my car, only used by a little old lady on Sundays . . .

Seriously speaking, software reuse is an intuitively appealing yet seductively elusive method for increasing programmer productivity and quality. The road to reuse is uphill, to say the least, and filled with numerous potholes, dead-ends, and blind alleys. Furthermore, the cost of reuse is significant (often 2–3 times greater than that of software designed for a single application).

The ultimate goal of this book is to provide a roadmap for the successful institutionalization of reuse. The reader is first introduced to various inhibitors and facilitators to software reuse (e.g., ego, intellectual property rights, programming language constructs, design techniques, etc.) through a series of humorous parables and anecdotes. The second half of the book provides details for overcoming these technical and nontechnical reuse inhibitors while avoiding the traps others have fallen into when trying to introduce software reuse programs into their organizations. Finally, I have included a detailed domain analysis process at the end of this book to address the questions: "What software should be made reusable?" and "How do you make software reusable?"

WHO SHOULD READ THIS BOOK?

You don't have to have ever written a program to enjoy reading this book (though some of the numerous puns that are strewn throughout this book

---

[1] Not really, I just wanted to say that because other people always write it and it really causes me to get all choked up inside—the same as when I watch the Buffalo Bills lose four straight Super

may not have the byte that they would if you had). This book was written for the entertainment and enlightenment of the general technical community. Current and future programmers will identify with the "challenges" they face slinging code. Systems engineers will reap satisfaction in the "I told you so" role they play in transitioning to a reuse program. Managers will especially benefit from the focus on the nontechnical issues, as well as learning from the failures and successes of others who have traveled down the reuse road.

In conclusion, read on! I hope you have as much fun reading this book as I had writing it. Besides, you might pick up a point or two that will help you save time and money by not "re-inventing" any wheels.

ACKNOWLEDGMENTS

First, I would like to thank IEEE Computer Society Press for giving me permission to (re)use some of the material in this book. Most of my "Confessions," which serve as the core material for the first few chapters of this book, have appeared in the *Open Channel* section of *IEEE Computer*. In addition, portions of this material, in a different format, have appeared in *Software Reuse: Emerging Technology* [Tra88b].

Second, I am indebted to the referees and members of the Addison-Wesley publication team for all they have done to improve the quality of the material in this book.

In addition, I would like to acknowledge the efforts of my esteemed peers in the field of software reuse whose papers, opinions, and personalities have influenced what you are about to read. I would also like to apologize to them for any "reuse" of ideas that inadvertently may have been included in this book without proper citation. But, then again, some of them have done it to me before, so now we are even. In particular, I would like to acknowledge Martin Griss—the self-proclaimed reuse rabbi,[2] Ted Biggerstaff—the founding father of software reuse, Ruben Prieto-Díaz—the founding faceted classifier, Jim Neighbors—the first father of domain analysis, David Parnas—

Bowls. Seriously, it was something I have been meaning to do for the last five years, which to me seems like a lifetime.

[2] I would especially like to thank Martin Griss, with whom I have been trading "horrid bed pans" (as he puts it) over the last several years. Just as punsters feed off of each other, in many ways, technically, we have nurtured each other's work and, in my humble opinion, the state of the art of reuse is better off for it (though it has been unfortunate for those individuals who have had to suffer through our punny presentations).

the heralder of change, Doug McIlroy—the software component industry visionary from Bell Labs, Bill Frakes, Jeff Poulin, Larry Latour, Sholom Cohen, Guillermo Arango, Sid Bailin, Bertrand Meyer, Don Batory, Lou Coglianese, Eric Newton, Masao Matsumoto, Sadahiro Isoda, Mitch Lubars, Ed Berard, Steve Edwards, and Joseph Goguen. I can without reservation recommend to the reader any material produced by this cast of reuse crusaders.

Finally, I would like to thank Woody Allen, whose wit and charm warped me at an early age. I would also like to thank Dr. David Lougee, my writing professor at Stanford University. His interesting lectures on the joys of lex taught me write from wrong.

Will Tracz
Owego, NY
tracz@lfs.loral.com
bxcd07a@prodigy.com

Prologue[1]

"Good Morning! Thank you for inviting me here today. I have to confess that I am looking forward to sharing the experience and insight I have gained working in the second oldest programming profession—that is "Second-Hand Software."

I confess, I am a used program salesman. This is true.

And, today is your lucky day! Such a deal! Such a deal I have for you! I happen to have some real *cream puffs* here that you might like to take out for a spin (i.e., a 9-track tape). This one was only driven on Sundays by a little old lady programmer.

Here we have some real classics (hold up deck of punch cards) that make great Christmas cards. Here is a vintage late model that makes a perfect gift at Christmas (hold up data cartridge). You know—"*a cartridge in a pear tree.*"

We also feature a fine selection of compacts (show 5¼ inch floppies) and subcompacts (show 3½ inch floppies).

And, if you act now, I will throw in one hundred feet of mylar tape *for free,* just perfect for trimming that Christmas tree!

So much for a trip down media memory lane.

As I was saying, I am a used program salesman. Over the last nine years, with tongue in cheek and pun in hand, I have written over a dozen "Confessions of a Used Program Salesman" that have appeared in *IEEE Computer, IEEE Software*, and *ACM SIGSOFT* (Association for Computer Machinery Special Interest Group in Software Engineering) *Software Engineering Notes.*

I remember vividly when I tried to get the first one published. It was right after one of those burn-out projects called AN-UK-43[2] (pronounced yuk!)—three months of twelve hour days and six day weeks. Projects like that tend to bring the best out in some people, or, if you happen to be a hot dog like I was,[3] the wurst. Anyway, when I took the paper to get it signed off, *I just about got*

---

[1] This is a transcript of an invited presentation given at Bell Northern Research Research Labs, Ottawa, Canada, December 3, 1991.

[2] What a name! Only the government could come up with a name like that!

[3] I relish thinking that I still can still cut the mustard, but the truth is that I find it harder and harder to ketchup with the newer kids on the block.

fired! It became obvious that not everyone at my place of employment shared my same taste (or lack of taste) for humor. But that didn't stop me. I published it anyway, on *April 1, 1983*,[4] an appropriate date if I do say so myself! I was very careful not to reveal my employer's name, using my home address only (never mind that my company was the only software employer in the city, let alone the whole county).

This pretense went on for years until I was interviewed by *Datamation* magazine for an article they were doing on software reuse. When I received a draft copy of the article, I was horrified! It seems that the article started out:

"According to Will Tracz, IBM's used program salesman . . . "[5]

I said, "W-A-I-T a minute!" I could imagine how well that would go over with the people in Armonk.

"So, I hear IBM is selling used programs! What's wrong with them? Why did someone dump this program? Or did it dump them (get it)?"

It suffices to say that I asked the writer to change the lead-in sentence a bit to read:

"One active proponent of reusability is Will Tracz, an advisory programmer at IBM's Federal Systems Div., Oswego [sic], NY.[6] A member of the company's Corporate Reuse Council, Tracz poses his "alter ego" as a used program salesman to draw attention to the issues surrounding software reuse."[7]

So, the cat is out of the bag. As careful as I have been to only include my home or academic address, not my work credentials, with every new confession someone has put two and two together and come up with one used program salesman, me. Grady Booch borrowed the title slightly once (he confessed to me later), but in my business imitation is the highest form of flattery, so I didn't really mind."

---

[4] April 1st is referred to as "April Fool's Day" in the U.S.—a day for practical joke playing.

[5] I should point out that I am no longer "IBM's used program salesman," but am now "Loral's used program salesman" because IBM sold the division I work for (the Federal Systems Division) to Loral in the spring of 1994.

[6] It is Owego, not Oswego, for those people who really care. Obviously the copy editors at *Datamation* never heard of Owego.

[7] *Datamation*, September 15, 1988.

Chapter 1

Introduction

"In order to reuse software, there needs to be software to reuse."

—Tracz [Tra88c]

SOFTWARE REUSE is a buzzword term that software managers and practitioners often pay lip service to without understanding its true implications or understanding how to structure an organization to leverage its potential effectively. The concept of software reuse has been part of the programming heritage since the origins of the stored program computer EDSAC at the University of Cambridge in 1949. Maurice Wilkes [Eam73] first recognized the need to avoid the redundant effort in writing scientific subroutines and recommended that a library of routines be kept for general use. Until recently, little had been done to extend program reusability beyond this rather simple level. McIlroy [McI69] in 1968 envisioned software component factories, but apparently only the Japanese listened. In May 1994, David Fisher [Fis94] at the National Institute of Standards and Technology (NIST) announced an "Advanced Technology Program Focused on Component-Based Software" whose business goals include "creation of systematically reusable software components." Unfortunately, during the last decade, although this simple, but effective concept of not reinventing the wheel has attracted much interest, it has resulted in more failure and frustration than success. As the NIST program suggests, we have a way to go.

The formidable "software crisis" [Boe81] in the light of impressive improvements in the price-to-processing-power ratio of hardware and advances in programming language design, compiler construction, and interactive graphics has forced software developers to reevaluate the trade-offs made in establishing the traditional ad hoc development methods and environments. New and better ways are being explored to harness these recent technological advances and to develop an integrated software/hardware system optimized for programmer productivity. Again and again the role of reusable software has been identified and discussed (e.g., see [DRR83, Ale86, Fre83, HM84, Jon84, Sta84, RH83].

The goal of this book is to entertain, educate, and enlighten (in that order) the reader about software reuse. It is the author's belief that in order for reuse to be institutionalized, the following issues[1] must be addressed:

1. getting top *management* support,

2. modifying the software development *process*,

3. overcoming *nontechnical* inhibitors,

4. creating *incentive programs* (carrot and stick),

5. establishing reuse *measurements*,

6. developing reuse *guidelines*, and

7. focusing on a *single domain* or application area.

Furthermore, based on personal experience, each of these areas *must* be addressed or the transition to a component-based software development process will not be realized. The material in this book serves as a basis for addressing each of these issues by first providing anecdotal insights into each and then providing technical directions to deal with them.

This chapter first establishes some common vocabulary that will be used throughout the book and then paints a broad picture of the issues related to software reuse. In particular the question *"Where does reuse start?"* is addressed by focusing on:

1. the *products* that can be reused,

2. the *processes* that need to be modified to support the development and utilization of reusable resources, and

3. the *personnel* that need to be motivated and educated if reuse is to have an impact on a particular organization.

The end of the chapter describes the organization of the rest of the material in this book.

---

[1] Adapted from the writings of the reuse rabbi, Martin Griss.

REUSE OVERVIEW

Software reuse is the type of thing some people swear by.[2] It is also the type of thing that some people swear at. Software reuse is a religion, a religion that not everyone has accepted and embraced to the degree I apotheosize. I do not claim to have experienced divine intervention. You don't need to take what I say as gospel truth. I believe in what I write, but what you read may be something different. The reader should note that the material in this book is intentionally redundant in that I am approaching the same topics from two different directions (anecdotally, with humor, and academically, without distraction). This overview is an informal introduction to topics that will be discussed in more detail in the chapters that follow.

Reuse Defined

Before I proceed further, I need to qualify software reuse by providing a definition.

- *Software reuse* is the process of reusing software that was designed to be reused.

- Software reuse is distinct from *software salvaging*, that is, reusing software that was not designed to be reused.

- Furthermore, software reuse is different than *carrying-over code*, that is, reusing code from one version of an application to another.

To summarize, *reusable software is software that was designed to be reused.*

An appealing analogy related to the evolution of software that further clarifies the definition of reuse looks at reuse as occurring across three dimensions:

1. Software evolution across *time* is *maintenance*, where one reuses (carries over) a previous version of an application as the basis for the next version of a program.

---

[2] The material in this section is based on my keynote address for the Reuse in Practice Workshop sponsored by the Institute for Defense Analysis (IDA), the Software Engineering Institute (SEI), and the Association of Computer Machinery Special Interest Group in Ada (SIGADA) in Pittsburgh, Pennsylvania, at the Software Engineering Institute (SEI), July 11–13, 1989.

2. Software evolution across *environments* is *porting*, where one reuses (carries over) a large portion of an existing application by changing only the portion necessary to get it to run on some other hardware platform or operating system.

3. Software evolution across *applications* is *true reuse* (as defined by the software reuse research community), where software is reused in an application other than that for which it was initially designed.

Where Does Reuse Start?

If I were to ask you, "Where does reuse start?," your reply might be, "What do you mean? That seems like a pretty vague and nebulous question!" I agree, so I have done a little top-down stepwise refinement and broken the question up to focus on three areas—the three P's of software reuse:

1. *product*, or what do we reuse,

2. *process*, or when do we apply reuse, and

3. *personnel*, or who makes reuse happen.

I guess I could have called it the three W's of reuse: *what*, *when*, and *who*.

"Why is this an important question?" you might ask. The first answer that comes to *my* mind is that if you would like to build a tool to help reuse software, it would be reasonable to know:

1. what you were trying to reuse,

2. when you would be doing it, and

3. who would be using it.

That is one reason, a pretty good reason, but not the only reason for asking the question "Where does reuse start?" Rhetorically, if one could understand the ramifications, implications, and economic justifications of the answer to the original question, "Where does reuse start?," one would better be able to answer the question "Where should reuse start?" and "What needs to be done to make it happen?" These are the real questions on which this book focuses.

Product

If one examines the question of "Where does reuse start?" by identifying the products being reused, one could ask "Does reuse *start* with code?" There is no denying that software reuse generally *ends* with "code." But this is still a pretty broad statement. After all, code could be source code, object code, a high-level language statement, a function, a procedure, a package, a module, or an entire program. The issue raised then is "What is the granularity of the code that you want to reuse?" The larger the granularity, the larger the "win" is in productivity (or so the perception is among programmers). The overhead for finding, understanding, and integrating a reusable software component needs to be less than that for designing and writing the code from scratch (again, such is the unrealistically optimistic perception of programmers who consistently underestimate the true "cost" of a line of code). This supports the argument for the reuse of higher granularity objects such as software packages, modules, or classes.

Just as we could debate the granularity of the object being reused, one could argue about the level of abstraction that is being manipulated. Does reuse start with a *design*? A design is a higher level abstraction compared to an implementation. Let me emphasize that the advantage of starting reuse from a design is that a design is at a higher level of abstraction than an implementation. Or, in other words, a design has fewer implementation details that constrain its applicability.

The two general rules of thumb for designing software to reuse are

1. separate *context* from *content* and *concept*,[3] and

2. factor out *commonality*, or to rephrase this second rule a bit, isolate *change*.

If one applies the first rule of thumb, a program design, say, at the detailed logic level, should have absent from it some (but not all) of the contextual information that will be supplied at implementation time. That is, the implementation issues, such as specific operating system or hardware dependencies, are not part of the content, which is the algorithm, or data flow, or part of the concept, which is the functional specification. I will address the second rule of thumb, factoring out commonality, later.

---

[3] For more information on this "3C" model, see [Tra90b].

Before proceeding, I would like to emphasize the importance of representation, especially from a tool perspective. I stated earlier that one of the reasons for looking for an answer to the question of "Where does reuse start?" was to provide a rationale for building tools to assist in the reuse process. This implies that we would like a machine manipulable reusable design representation. This is not easy! But I believe that the state of the art is now evolving to a point where there are results of software reuse starting from design. The DESIRE [Lub87] system at MCC is an early example. Another example is the 50 Steps per Module system (50SM) at Toshiba [MFYO87] where they are working on an expert system [HSH+86] to generate automatically C, FORTRAN, or Ada from low-level design data-flow charts. Furthermore, they claim success in reverse engineering of existing software by synthesizing data-flow diagrams for potential reuse.

Continuing our analysis of the question "Where does reuse start?," could reuse start with a program's *specification*? By specification, I mean a statement of "what" a program needs to do, not "how" it is supposed to do it. There is a simple answer: yes. In limited contexts, program specifications can be reusable. But research in automatic programming tells us this is a hard problem to extrapolate outside of narrow domains.

Speaking from personal experience, at Loral Federal Systems in Owego, New York (formerly IBM Federal Systems Division), they have developed some reusable avionics specifications [BG90] [i.e., MIL-STD-2167 System Requirements Specifications (SRS)].[4] These specifications are highly parameterized documents full of empty tables and missing parameter values. The systems analyst, in effect, programs a new module by specifying the values in the tables of the SRS document. An application generator then reads the document and builds the data structures necessary to drive the supporting software.

Continuing our backward walk through the waterfall model, we can ask the question about whether reuse can start with a problem definition *(requirements)*. This is an interesting question. One might ask "How?" One could reason that if the same requirements can be identified as being satisfied by certain previously developed modules, then clearly those modules are candidates for preuse. Well, that is a big "if." It is significantly dependent on the traceability of requirements to specifications, the traceability of specifications to design, and the traceability of design into code and also into *test cases* and *documentation*.

---

[4] These are "informal" specifications. For a discussion on software reuse and "formal specifications," see [MMM94].

Here is where a hypertext system's information web is ideal for linking these artifacts. With a hypertext system, you can walk the beaten path to find out what code to reuse. But there is a catch. As Ted Biggerstaff has repeatedly stated, there is no free lunch [Tra88a]. You have to pre-engineer the artifacts to fit into the network, and spend the time and effort to create the links.[5] Finally, you somehow need to separate the context of the objects from the content. One mechanism for achieving this goal is through parameterization. *Parameterization* is a way to extend the domain of applicability [PD87] of reusable software. Parameterization allows a single module to be generalized over a set of solutions.

To summarize, the issue we have been exploring related to the question of "Where does reuse start?" is really the question "What software artifact does reuse start with?" Part of the answer lies in the fact that we know that software reuse generally *ends* with the reuse of code. Where it starts depends on

1. how much effort we want to place in developing the reusable artifact that we want to begin with,

2. how effectively we can link it to an implementation, and

3. (maybe not so obvious) how effectively we generalize the implementation.

Reflecting on the generalization issue of an implementation, one must recognize that as we progress down the waterfall model, from requirements to implementation, each artifact adds more detail. An implementation is one instantiation[6] of a design. There could be several implementations of a design just as there could be several designs that satisfy a specification but that have different performance and resource attributes. The key is factoring out the commonality by separating the context from the concept and content. The *concept* becomes the functional specification. The *content* becomes a template or generic object. The *context* becomes possible instantiation parameters.

We have identified some of the dimensions and implications related to which software artifact to start reuse with. I have concluded that code is a safe

---

[5] Although today tools (e.g., DOMAIN [HTN94]) exist that can help automate the hypertext link creation using lexigraphical pattern matching.

[6] *Instantiation* is the process of substituting values for parameters in macros, code templates, Ada generic packages, or other parameterized modules.

place to start and is, in most cases, the place one ends up. I have also mentioned that hypertext is the way to establish the traceability between requirements, specification, design, tests, and implementation.

Process

Turning to the software development process, one could observe that most software reuse starts at the *implementation* phase. One could modify the software development process to include a step where, at implementation time, one would look for existing software to save having to write new code that would do the same thing. With a little luck, this usually works. But with a little foresight, this usually works much better. How often is it the case that the code one wants to reuse has to be modified because either it was not implemented to fit exactly the new context in which it is being reused, or it was not implemented to provide a parameter for adapting it to a different context, or the design was such that it placed unnecessary constraints on the implementation? If the software designer had not placed the (somewhat) arbitrary design constraints in the initial design, then the implementation could be used as is.

Therefore, with a little foresight, reuse might better start at *design* time. The implementor could then leverage off the functionality of existing implementations. This is where the bottom-up aspect of reuse meets the top-down functional decomposition aspect of most design processes. One could argue that object-oriented design [Mey87] would eliminate this problem. Let me say that, in my opinion, object-oriented design helps reduce the problem of the design not meeting the implementation, but parameterization is still the key for controlling this process.

One could just as easily extend the same argument for looking for reuse opportunities at design time, for the same reasons, to the *specification* and *requirements analysis* phases of the software life cycle. Again, by identifying what is available to be reused earlier in the software development life cycle, trade-offs can be made in the specifications, or designs can be tailored to leverage the existing software base.

Let me now introduce a new phase to the traditional waterfall model; a phase that has been added explicitly to support software reuse. I define *domain analysis* [PD87] to be a generalization of requirements analysis—instead of analyzing the requirements for a specific application, the requirements of a generic application are quantified over a domain. Applying my two rules of thumb, commonality is factored out and context is separated from concept and content. Reusable objects are identified and their context defined. (An

example of the application of these two rules of thumb can be found in the domain engineering process contained in Appendix A.)

If one recognizes that the software development life cycle needs to be modified in order to inject software reuse technology, then, relating to personal experience, reuse opportunities and potential can be identified at *code review time* or at *design review time*.

If one looks at the Programming Process Architecture [PPA91] used at IBM, one can see these criteria called out as being integral parts of the inspection process.

But then again, instead of reuse being addressed during the software development effort, maybe reuse could start as an afterthought *(project follow-on)*. After one pass through the software development life cycle, the second time through one can begin to see the commonality between applications. Quoting Ted Biggerstaff's rules of three [Tra88a], "If you have not built three real systems in a particular domain, you are unlikely to be able to derive the necessary details of the domain required for successful reuse in that domain."

As a side point, there is a second rule of three. "Before you can reap the benefits of reuse, you need to reuse it three times." The empirical evidence I have seen to date bears this out.

A better choice for where reuse should start is at the beginning of a project *(project start-up)*. Here, the software development process can be defined, reusable software libraries can be set up, and standards and tools can be developed.

To share with you again my personal experience, in one large Ada project, a Computer Integrated Manufacturing (CIM) effort involving 350K SLOCS [LP91], the project had a PRL—project reuse lead. The PRL (pronounced "pearl") was responsible for sitting in on all design and specification reviews to identify commonality between subsystems and support the communication and application of reuse technology. Because of software reuse and the factoring out of commonalities, the size and development effort of the project was reduced by more than 20%. This is a successful example of where reuse started at the beginning of a project.

But, then again, maybe reuse could start at the end of a project *(project wrap-up)*. I am reminded of the General Dynamics approach for developing reusable software related to an early version of the DARTS system [MR83]. Here, after a project was completed, and before the design and development team was assigned to a new project, they locked everyone up in a room and wouldn't let them out until they developed an "archetype" of the system. That is, they recorded how and what to modify in the system so that it could be reused in the future. This is one approach for developing reusable software, but it seems like one is putting the cart in front of the horse. But then again, it is reasonable, on the completion of any project, to identify likely components to add to a reuse library.

Finally, we are all in this for the bottom line. Let me state my version of the Japanese software factory's motto: "Ask not what you can do for your software, but what your software can do for you."[7] It makes sense, dollars and cents, to capitalize on existing software resources and expertise. But you need to develop a *business case* to justify the additional cost of developing reusable software.

To summarize, the issue we have just explored related to the question of "Where does reuse start?" is really the question "Where in the software development life cycle does reuse start?" Where it starts depends on

1. how one modifies the software development process to identify opportunities for reuse, and

2. how one either modifies or extends the software life cycle to identify objects to make reusable.

Personnel

Turning to the last dimension I identified related to the question of "Where does reuse start?," we now focus on the key players in the reuse ball game. The first player to come to bat is the programmer. Does reuse start with a *programmer*? Most programmers are responsible for the design and implementation of software. If they can identify a shortcut to make their job easier, or to make them "appear" more productive to management, then they will probably be motivated to reuse software. But, although programmers might be inclined to reuse software if it was fun, or it was the path of least resistance, or they are told to, the real issue is "Who is going to create the software to reuse in the first place?" There needs to be a *critical mass*[8] of quality software for programmers to draw on in order for them to fully subscribe to the reuse paradigm! So, how do we bootstrap the system?

---

[7] With apologies to John F. Kennedy.

[8] This is not meant to be a religious statement! Furthermore, I am trying to get some kind of reaction, albeit, not nuclear. Having a depository of software "components" with nothing in it or with random quality and documentation does more to discourage reuse than encourage it.

Maybe *managers* can instill a more altruistic attitude in their programmers. This, of course, becomes a question of budget cost and schedule risks associated with the extra time and effort needed to make things reusable. (See Reuse Myth #3 in Chapter 17 for a discussion of the cost of reuse.)

Because reuse is a long-term investment, maybe the expense of developing reusable software should be spread across a *project*! With reuse raised to the project level, the potential for a larger return on investment would be higher, and we would gain more insight and experience in prioritizing what should be made reusable. Again, there is no free lunch [Tra88a]. A project manager would have to authorize the cost. But project management is generally rewarded for getting a job done on time and under budget. There is no motivation for making the next project look good. Neither is there any motivation to make any other project within the organization look good. This shortsighted outlook needs to be resolved with *top management*.

Indeed, this is the case, both here and abroad. At NTT, GTE, IBM, and TRW, to name a few companies, reuse incorporation and deposition objectives are being set. For instance, at NTT, top management has set a reuse ratio goal of 20% on all new projects, with a deposition ratio quota of 5%. That is, all new programs ideally should consist of at least 20% source code from the reuse library and all new programs should try and deposit at least 5% of their source code into the reuse library (subject to the acceptance guidelines, constraints, and ultimate approval of the Reuse Committee).

But upper management ordering reuse to happen does not ensure success. That is why there is a strong argument for reuse to start in the classroom *(with the educator)*. The education system, although good at teaching theory, should embrace a little more engineering discipline and teach software building block construction or the "composition" of programs. Courses are needed in domain analysis, application generator construction, and parameterized programming, and prefabricated, off-the-shelf components structured to facilitate the construction of new applications in a classroom setting need to be made available. Again, critical mass is needed to bootstrap the system.

Besides the reuse mind-set, maybe reuse should start with a tool set *(with the tool developer)*. Personally, I do not see the need for exotic and elaborate tools to support reuse, although I am biased toward using a multimedia hypertext system for the capture and representation of domain knowledge, which I consider crucial to understanding what and how to reuse software.

Have I run out of people who possibly could start the reuse ball rolling? Have I saved my heavy hitters for last? You bet I have! Continuing on, should reuse start with the *customer*? Well, it depends on the customer! A large customer, like the Department of Defense, could easily demand certain reuse requirements be met. Of course, there might be a small initial overhead cost associated with getting the ball rolling, but once the system was primed, once application domains were populated with certified, parameterized, well-documented, reusable components, then long-term benefits could be reaped. [This is the motivation for the ARPA-funded Domain-Specific Software Architecture (DSSA) Program.]

I have added the *salesperson* to this list of individuals who could play a role in determining where reuse might start. If a salesperson knows the marketplace and knows potential customers, then they could play a key role in building the business case necessary to justify the capitalization of software for reuse. What better argument to justify building reusable software components if you know there are customers for whom applications can be built using these parts.

Finally, I have added the *systems analyst* as being a person who possibly could be instrumental in starting software reuse. I admit, he joined the team late, but he turns out to be a clutch player. Back to the issue of putting the horse in front of the cart. Before you can reuse software, you need software to reuse. Who are you going to call? The domain analysts! Who are the most qualified individuals in an organization to

1. analyze a problem domain,

2. determine logical subsystems and functions, and

3. determine the contents or requirements of modules and anticipate the different contexts under which they might be applied?

The systems analysts, under most circumstances, are the right people to do this job, although they have made life so difficult for some of us programmers in the past by providing incomplete, inconsistent, or, worse yet, too detailed specifications. This is a wonderful opportunity to work together toward a common goal.

To summarize, the issue we have been exploring related to the question of "Where does reuse start?" has been identifying the roles played by certain individuals in an organization related to making software reuse happen. In retrospect, several of the key players have nontechnical roles! This is a point that bears distinction and should come as no surprise.

ORGANIZATION OF THIS BOOK

I have probably raised more questions in the preceding material than I have answered, but that is good. I hope I have whetted your appetite to find out more details about how you can avoid the costly mistakes others have made in trying to institutionalize software reuse.

As you can deduce from the preface and this informal reuse overview, I have been enjoying "opun" season on the programming profession for the last ten years, taking potshots at whatever struck my funny bone, or other parts of my anatomy. At the same time, I have published extensively on both the technical and nontechnical issues related to software reuse [Tra86, Tra87a, Tra87b, Tra87c, Tra87d, Tra88b, Tra88c, Tra89, Tra90a, Tra90b, Tra91a, Tra93a, Tra93b, Tra93c]. Most recently, besides serving as chair or cochair of three workshops on software reuse, I was involved in setting up the reuse program for the entire IBM Corporation [TG93]. In addition, I have been involved as a principal investigator (PI) for ARPA's DSSA program [Met90, GM92, CST92], which is focused on defining and refining the technology, processes, and infrastructure necessary to support large-scale reuse.

In the following pages, I provide a collection of my rascally ramblings as well as some serious chapters on how one can successfully implement a reuse program. Most of the former offerings fall under the category of "Confessions." Others are just pithy revelations of the same genre. Each piece is followed by a Background section giving some anecdotal insights into the circumstances that led up to its creation and/or some repercussions of having it appear in print. In addition, scattered throughout the book are several Soapbox sections in which I have chosen to inject various opinions/opunions of interest. This introduces the reader to several important reuse-related topics including the following:

Chapter 2:   documentation and modularization,
Chapter 3:   language features that support reuse (Ada),
Chapter 4:   general programming language issues,
Chapter 5:   reuse motivators,
Chapter 6:   technology transition,
Chapter 7:   reuse inhibitors,
Chapter 8:   acquisition of reusable assets,
Chapter 9:   design of reusable software,
Chapter 10:   the influence of technology on reuse,
Chapter 11:   the cost of reuse,

Chapter 12:   reuse education,
Chapter 13:   reuse legal issues,
Chapter 14:   reuse research,
Chapter 15:   design reuse, and
Chapter 16:   reuse theology/technology.

On the serious side, the second half of the book provides more technical information on how to avoid the pitfalls and potholes of institutionalizing a software reuse program in an industrial setting. Although there is some redundancy in content with the material found in the first 16 chapters, this is meant to provide reinforcement and more detail.[9]

Chapter 17 is an expanded version of the following "Software Reuse Myths," which I wrote more than five years ago:

1. Software reuse is only a *technical* problem.

2. *Special tools* are needed for software reuse.

3. The reuse of code results in *huge increases* in productivity.

4. *Artificial intelligence* will solve the reuse problem.

5. The *Japanese* have solved the reuse problem.

6. *Ada or C++* has solved the reuse problem.

7. Designing *software* from reusable parts is like designing *hardware* using integrated circuits.

8. *Reused* software is the same as *reusable* software.

9. Software reuse *will just happen*.

The chapter now revisits each original myth and evaluates each premonition against recent advances in the states of the art.

Chapter 18 provides more detail on reuse inhibitors—the technical and nontechnical barriers to software reuse—and on motivators—the direct and indirect benefits to reuse.

Chapter 19 contains a list of reuse technical directions. This material identifies which emerging technologies will have the most impact on software

---

[9]The other reason for the overlap is that not everyone may appreciate my sense of humor (not that reuse is a laughing matter). The second half of the book provides a more traditional textbook presentation of the material.

reuse. The last chapter uses a reuse maturity model to help the reader evaluate what reuse potential their organization currently has and helps them chart a path to improving their reuse levels.

Finally, included as an appendix, is a domain analysis/engineering process that provides details on how reusable resources can be identified and how they can be organized to maximize their domain of applicability and adaptability resulting in improving their chances of reuse.

SUMMARY

A wise old owl once posed to his son (who kept saying "what" all the time), "Son, it's not 'what'! You know? It's 'who'! You know?" Software reuse is no exception to this rule. Software reuse is a people issue as well as a technology issue.

The material in this book is both an anecdotal reflection of the growth of the programming profession projected through the eyes and ears of your "friendly used program salesman" as well as a reference to those wishing to institute a reuse program. The technical foundations for making software reuse a viable alternative to program development have been identified and demonstrated, thus adding credibility to the used program business. Reuse is not a reality for us all, but the question of whether or not it is—and always will be—the technology of the future has been answered by the material in the book.

Chapter 2

My First Confession

I AM a used program salesman. My profession is probably one of the oldest yet most overlooked in the software industry today. My glory is not in creating shiny new systems; I'm often delegated to brushing up an old clunker with a new coat of paint. I was not always a refurbisher of programs; once I aspired to be a great creator of wonderful and complex systems. Fresh out of graduate school, I entered the job market ready to apply my expertise to solve all the world's problems. Too soon after accepting my first job I realized the completely inexplicable reluctance of management to unleash the super programmer lurking in a naive and humble employee like me.

My baptism into the used program business occurred right after my training period. I was assigned to the task of modifying a punch tape program, and I remember the zeal with which I attacked my first "real" program. I also remember, not as pleasantly, how I took two days to recover from the impact of trying to read that "REAL" (wretched would be a better word) code. Talk about a bowl of spaghetti. Being innocent and naive I thought self-modifying code was the exception, not the norm. The comments, what few appeared, were classics like "DO IT TO IT" and "IN MEMORY OF JIM AND GLEN." But this assignment was just the start, and after many more patch-and-paste jobs I began to catch on. I soon adopted the strategy of rewriting more and modifying less. I saw the light of modularization and was saved by the hand of documentation. Gradually I budgeted more for program improvement to go along with program modification.

Then, one cold and dark December day I took the bull by the horns and accepted an assignment that was to change my destiny. Instead of producing the delivered program by modifying an existing program, I created a new baseline, applying all my skill and modern programming practice. From then on, I had it made; customers beat a path to my door, knowing that I could produce more and better at a greater speed and for less. My ego was once again properly inflated. I had become the best used program salesman on my block;

but that is not the end of my story. There is a moral to be told, a lesson to be learned.

In all seriousness, the used program business is a realistic and practical aspect of the software industry today. Quite simply, we don't "reinvent the wheel" every time we develop new programs. Time and money are our major constraints. Often we are faced with a schedule or budget that forces us to work smarter not harder. Here is where good programming practice pays off.

When systems are properly modularized, documented, and debugged, and have all the other good things done to them, they can be used as basic components of, or building blocks, for other systems. I learned the merits of modular strength and coupling, not in Comp Sci 406, "Introduction to Used Program Sales," but from the school of hard knocks. It is a program modification lesson I have taken to heart, a lesson that has helped me increase my productivity—which, in turn, has increased the productivity of those who use my software.

BACKGROUND

This was my first attempt at satire.[1] It was motivated by Edsger Dijkstra's ACM Turing Award Lecture, "The Humble Programmer" [Dij82]. I am a product of my environment. I came in at the grungiest level of programming, into an industry that was still faced with space, weight, and cost constraints. This was where real men coded in binary with switches (actually, it was in hex using a hexadecimal keypad, which I guess showed the progress we had made at the time). On a good day, card punches and paper tape were par for the course, and I was lucky to get two or three turnarounds on my jobs before going into the lab to debug on second shift. In graduate school,[2] I had similarly slaved over punch card machines and worshiped the insides of operating

---

[1] In my undergraduate writing classes I had tended toward this writing style (a bit sarcastic and irreverent—don't ask me about the protest song I wrote that is probably on file someplace in Washington, D.C.), but it must not have been appreciated by my writing instructor because, even though I received mostly A's on all assignments, I received a C in the course because, in my professor's words, "I never improved."

[2] I should qualify this, since I have been to three different graduate schools; Penn State (1972–1974, masters of computer science and keypunch operation), Syracuse (1974–1979, masters of electrical and computer engineering), and Stanford (1987–199?, for a Ph.D. in electrical engineering). I might justifiably be called a "perpetual grad student," but I prefer "techno-maven." Of course, I have been called a "techno-nerd" sometimes too, but I would rather not discuss that right now. The bottom line is that I hope to graduate from college before my oldest son graduates.

systems. I also got to twiddle some microcode (in octal) to make our graphics processor in the lab stand up and dance.

I published this article without acknowledging my employer because, at the time, it might have been interpreted as being irreverent to the point of jeopardizing my career. That is not to say that the people I worked for didn't have a sense of humor. Some did, and others just didn't have one like mine. When I saw it in print, I must admit it really felt good, and when I didn't get fired, or even mildly reprimanded, I was even happier, though I didn't go out of my way to tell anyone about it.

SOAPBOX: WHAT'S THE USE?

Did you ever stop to wonder why software is the only "engineering discipline" (and I use both words loosely) besides waste water management to include "reuse" in its vocabulary? Other true engineering disciplines build new systems by simply "using" standardized, off-the-shelf components. Furthermore they base their designs on analytical models. Unfortunately, the software engineering profession is not mature enough to have the collected wisdom and insight to develop these architectural models. Similarly, there has been little economic incentive to create (re)usable components, partially due to legal issues regarding copyright infringement.

For a more detailed treatment of this topic see Software Myth #7 in Chapter 17.

Chapter 3

An Update from
My First Confession

IN THE four years that passed since I wrote my first confession in 1982, something happened to the used program business. While I was busy basking in that warm glow of success that stemmed from finding a way not to reinvent the wheel each time I had to get a product out the door, it seems that a new lady came into town with an even better bag of tricks.

At first I couldn't quite figure out the exact orientation of the object she was peddling. The banter and hoopla that surrounded this universal elixir of hers was confounded by the reported complexity and sheer immensity of the instructions that came with it. Furthermore, the manufacturer's track record was suspect, although the formula they were using consisted of elements of known therapeutic value. Were they in the right proportions? How easy were they to use? How did they all fit together? I decided to investigate.

I scheduled a rendezvous with her and, I must admit, was a bit taken aback by her massive size and frills, but "You can't judge a book by its cover," I always say, and, besides, she seemed to have all the right stuff in the places that really mattered. I was most interested in her bag of tricks, which, she said, contained objects that I would find of value in perpetuating my trade of selling used programs. What she pulled out were packages. Not just ordinary packages, like the kind you get on your birthday where you have to guess what is inside. These packages had an envelope on the top of each one that specified what was inside them. Like a flash, I could see the writing on the wall, but in reality it was her writing on those envelopes that lit the fire. I could use the packages as building blocks without looking inside them by just referencing the envelopes for instructions on how to use what was inside. No more looking under the hood of every used program to see what was inside and how to use it. I could just keep a file of each of these so-called package specifications around to reference.

I asked her what other kinds of talents she had. She told me she was good at juggling, too. Her bag of tricks had some special packages tailored for doing two things at once. I was impressed at the thought, since there were many of my used programs I could speed up given a mechanism and facility for concurrency. I could run on two four-cylinder engines instead of a V8 and keep my customers happy.

After this we were making small talk when I asked her if she had any other classy objects to show. She said there was one other package she hadn't shown. I asked her what type it was. She said it was a do-it-yourself type; that I could make it into any type I wanted and it would perform the same function. At first, I was skeptical. How could there be such a generalized routine? But she showed me several instances and I was convinced.

So where does that leave our young hero? What is a gentleman to do? This casual relationship with the lady has turned into a full-fledged courtship. I have fully embraced her way of packaging, and she has taught me to juggle. I am working on a new set of packages to help me in the used program business, and I will keep you posted on how they turn out. I have learned that while you can't always judge a book by its cover, you can pretty well always judge a package by its specification. Ada is, at first look, a complex lady whose reputation has been tarnished by accusations that she is part of the problem, rather than the solution to the software crisis (see "The Emperor's Old Clothes," *CACM*, Vol. 24, No. 2, February 1981). From personal experience, I can honestly say that while she is still a little rough around the edges, she is a welcome partner in the quest for reusable software (the so-called used programs that I purport to sell).

BACKGROUND

Where were you when you first heard about Ada [Ada83]? I had been hacking around in PL/I for five years and when the company I was working for saw the writing on the wall—according to the little green book[1]—I was selected for "proper indoctrination." This was back in 1984, when the dust was just settling and the tools they called compilers were mere shadows of things to come.

---

[1] This is an insider joke about Ada, whose Language Reference Manual is green and not so little. I would also like to point out that it is, in my opinion, the most intellectually disturbing book I have ever read. Too bad it wasn't written in English (another insider joke). Also, I would like to offer an apology to any readers that may have been offended by the sexist nature of my analogy. It was obviously influenced by the prevailing military mindset at the time it was written.

I fell in love with modularization and parameterized types, having been a big IBM Assembler H Macro man and PL/I Pre-Processor proponent, these features suited my modus operandi—sort of. I was still frustrated by the lack of good bit/byte twiddling operations and the fact that parameterization was a bit awkward (not to mention the generated code a bit slow), but these things were easily overcome by rolling my own bit/byte manipulation packages and using the C (or whatever I could get my hands on) preprocessor to allow me to do some conditional compilation—albeit outside the language, but who cares anyway?

I was fortunate to hook up with some Ada gurus (Geoff Mendall and Doug Bryan) during my stay at Stanford and they helped me along. One interesting event, which occurred in 1986 while I was at Stanford, happened at a Computer Science Forum open house. Forum members from Japan had come to my research group for a demonstration of the Ada formal specification tools we were building. After the demo, they showed us the output of a dependency analysis tool they had written for Ada programs. I commented, after studying the diagram, that I didn't know they were writing software in Ada. They said they weren't; in fact, they didn't even have an Ada compiler for the machine they were developing the software for. Perplexed, I asked them why they were interested in Ada. Their reply was very thought provoking. They said they were using Ada as a design language because of the tasking model (concurrency) it supported. They felt that with the trend toward decreasing costs for microprocessors, new applications soon would be migrated to multiprocessor-based systems and they didn't want to have to redesign their software. With their software in Ada, they could reuse their designs, while debugging their designs with existing computing platforms. Furthermore, the separation of interface from implementation was the perfect vehicle for "black box" reuse, which they supported.

The bottom line is that the best place to start leveraging reuse is at design time and that Ada packages support this approach.

Postscript.   Ada did not stop in 1983. It has since gone on to new and better things in the form of Ada 9X [Ada89]. Although most of the improvements in Ada 9X center on the tasking model, there are a couple nice features that support reuse: a form of polymorphism through variant records and the ability to treat packages as types.

Chapter 4

The Loves in My Life

BEING IN the used program business, you see all kinds, from slim, sleek, and sexy, to obese, clumsy, and unmanageable. As I say, "You can't judge a program by its user manual," so I always look under the hood to see what language it is written in before I consider adding it to my bag of tricks. Over the years, I must admit to having shopped around and to having brief encounters with various ladies of the languages,[1] some only intermittently, on a casual basis, some more passionately, lasting over periods of years, and some were, dare I say, just blind dates that I could hardly wait to dump (only to end up having them dump me all too often). Where should I start this torrid tale of tempestuous infatuation, but with my first affair of the heart.

The lab computer in my freshman physics class comes to mind as the logical FOCAL point. It was there that I made my first BASIC moves trying to communicate with a mini. As naive as I was, to me she was the most "simulating" thing I could get my hands on. I felt exhilarated when she let me tickle the keys on her TTY, and was spellbound by the pulsating rhythm of her response.

All too soon she was gone, replaced by her more mature bigger sister. I had to put all my cards on the table for this one, otherwise I was in for a batch of trouble. I must admit the courtship was a bit awkward because I could seldom get my hands on her. Instead, for the most part, we corresponded, like pen pals. To make matters worse, it was always a job to get to her since I had to

---

[1] *Warning:* The analogy being used in the following material is blatantly sexist and may offend almost as many readers as it amuses! It was written at a time in my life when society's norms were different than they are today. I had no awareness I would be offending anyone when I wrote it. I have chosen to include it here because it affords the reader not only some of the best punishment in the book, but it is almost a computer language trivia contest to see how many puns one can pick out of the languages being mentioned.

give my cards to her father (a smooth operator) who controlled how and when I could talk to her and take her out. To further confound the situation, he had a unique language and vocabulary. I can remember with frustration how I always had to type the specific directions on cards for him (so that he could tell what to do if *SYS* was *IN* or *OUT*).[2]

Where do we go to from here? Let's C; that's not it, for she is another story. My next fling occurred during summer vacation. I was doing some work around the computer center when my boss introduced us. She was all business, with many interesting features, but too bulky for my scientific style. I could read her like a book, but she was just too wordy. I soon grew tired of having to use so many words to say so little. I tried going out with her younger cousin, but have to report that she didn't generate (RPG) much interest—she turned out to be too formal. Then I met the apple of my AI (APL of my eye?), the first girl who I could actually interact with, and boy did we get it online. What strong and powerful features she had, and I could express so much by saying so little. Alas, the romance ended too soon, when I was distracted by a girl who spoke with a LISP. Little did I know what she symbolized. I felt manipulated and cursed repeatedly when I found out she was just stringing me along. Like unbalanced parentheses, we did not match. [Besides she had an annoying habit of collecting garbage at inopportune times and would always ask *could her* (CDR) brother borrow the *CAR*.]

Then one wintery day, I SLIPped into one of my old flames. She introduced me to her roommate, and the relationship just SNOWBALled. We burned a lot of CPU cycles together, as our patterns seemed to match, but our affair was scheduled for termination, all too soon, when I left for graduate school and warmer climates.

Working as a research assistant in the computer center I was quickly seduced by the dark side of software, that of system programming. Absolute power corrupts absolutely. I could never be HASPier. Soon I became a binary bigot, twiddling bits and going to wild parties where they put their keys on the table and actually swapped PSWs. What sleek and sexy programs I had assembled under my control, and the tricks they let me do were obscene, I am embarrassed to admit (although standards back then were a lot less formal than they are today). Needless to say, I had a BAL. Little did I know that this seductive wench was leading me down the road to ruin—five years went

---

[2] For those of you who have never experienced the joys of Job Control Language (JCL), which this comment is about, consider yourselves lucky!

by before I realized it. My used program lot filled up with top-of-the-line roadsters that could leave the competition stacked up in the ready wait queue while they finished the job in one time slice. Besides getting the job done in fewer cycles, they were easy on the core space too. What more could a customer ask for? A software sports car; compact, sleek, and efficient; optimized for speed.

The only problem was they didn't sell that well—not everyone spoke their language. Trouble also began when the customers that did speak the language decided they wanted to be their own mechanics. When they started monkeying around with what was under the hood, things got pretty messy, and soon I was spending more time in the shop repairing other people's programs than working on new models to add to my line. I realized, in my macroscopic view of the world, that I was addressing a more limited marketplace than I wanted too. In addition, it was taking me a year and a day to crank out a new program. Not everyone needed these high-performance features. There were bankers and scientists who would settle for a more general utility, which basically got the job done, without necessarily squeezing out those last few MIPS of performance. Furthermore, there were those that preferred the luxury models; the more fancy (though often useless) the options, the better. Finally, technology was catching up to me, memory prices were dropping and program size was virtually becoming a nonexistent problem.

The lights finally lit up like a blaze when I met the high-class debutante PASCAL on campus one day. We spoke on a much higher level than I did with my machine roommates. I could see she was a simple girl, for her vocabulary was quite limited and she was also quite picky, always checking the type of data we were talking about. At first, I found this quite annoying, but quickly saw the error in my ways. When I realized that I had spent the last five years of my life running around with those low-level lovelies, and I could have written my whole bag of used programs in one year with this new girl as my companion, I quickly converted.

Still, there was a bit missing in my life. What bugged me was that I always wanted to byte off more than I could chew. When I left school, I met an older, more mature woman, who told me she could help me eliminate my problem once and for all. She told me she was the one (PL/I), although I did not think I was the first. She had a lot of the features of my old flame, but was not as fussy with the type of data we talked about. Little did I realize what a complex person she really was. It turns out there were many ways I could tell her the same thing, but sometimes it took her longer to work it out. I was quickly seduced when she let me twiddle her bits and push some characters around. (Shades of my low-level days.) A working relationship existed between the two of us. During the next seven years, we got to know each other quite well. Occasionally, I confess, I would go forth and engage in some Smalltalk with others; I even logged some time with a pro(log), but for the most part I stayed pretty close to home.

Then one day, the older sister of my first high-level love graduated from military school (Ada). It was a big deal. I had read a lot about her and decided it might be nice to set up a rendezvous. The rest is history. We hit it off just swell. I loved her lace and frills, and we have been going steady ever since.

The lessons that I learned from this not atypical exposure to various programming languages is that there is a time and an application for all programming languages. Furthermore, I am a better person for having played the field. I realize now there are definite advantages in choosing a high-level language, especially in terms of productivity and portability. The requirements of tight, efficient code are no longer as important in most applications; therefore, resorting to my assembly language programming bag of tricks is seldom necessary (although quite handy for understanding implementation trade-offs). Besides, some compilers (but not as many as I would like) do generate some pretty good code (although sometimes you can fall asleep waiting).

Note: Portability is one of the cornerstones of reusable software. History shows that the smaller the program, the easier it is to maintain (in general). These factors, and others, have converted me to the high-level language Ada to base all my used programs on (reusable software).

P.S. In real life I have a new love. She is a cute baby girl who is worth a million, that is why we named her Meg.

BACKGROUND

In this chapter, I have made explicit the list of programming language puns that are strewn throughout. The original did not have such "clues," but I felt that some of the references might be pretty obscure, or IBM-centric, therefore, the average reader might miss them. While the reuse theme is not prevalent throughout the chapter, it is raised at the end by focusing on issues of portability versus efficiency.

In closing, there are two anecdotes that bear mentioning:

1. I published this article in *ACM Software Engineering Notes* because it was too long for *IEEE Computer*.

2. My daughter, Megan, was really born one month before I wrote this article and she continues to be priceless (as are my other children, Matt and Nick, which is something my wife would be quick to remind me of).

Chapter 5

Fringe Benefits

I JUST have to tell you about a strange phenomenon that has been happening in my used program business. Ever since I have been reusing some special parts to refurbish programs, my maintenance work has dropped off dramatically. I have had to shift my personnel around down at the body shop by placing more workers in manufacturing and fewer in repair. Quite frankly, it has been a drain financially, because more than half my revenue in the past has come from maintenance.

On the bright side, my reputation for delivering defect-free products has increased the number of customers I serve. I don't mind the shift in work-load—and to tell you the truth, my workers don't mind it either—for two reasons. First, manufacturing software with reused parts is a lot more fun than maintaining software. Second, maintenance now requires less effort. It is easier to find bugs because they are almost never in the special parts or building blocks that we have been reusing in each product, but almost always in the glue that holds the parts together. Finally, new products get easier to assemble from these components as we become more familiar with the components. We are constantly salvaging new software pieces to add to our parts warehouse whenever a new program to refurbish comes into the factory. Business is booming. (Now, if I could only figure out a way to recoup my lost mainte-nance revenue. Actually, I am thinking about going into the parts distribution business, but I haven't worked out the economic and legal issues yet.)

Seriously, one of the fringe benefits of software reuse is that the quality of the delivered product is increased. Reusable software components—in particular, components designed for reuse—generally have a very low defect rate. Furthermore, with each successful use, a component's confidence factor increases, as does the confidence of the programmer who reuses the component. Indeed, the saying that "one way to eliminate software bugs is by not putting them there in the first place" supports building software from reused parts. Actually, I should make a distinction between "plain parts" (the old subroutine library) and "reusable parts" (highly parameterized generic packages), but that is a topic for another true confession.

BACKGROUND

Quality clearly also plays a pivotal role in software reuse. There is a saying along the banks of the Hudson River that "The last reusable component you use is the first one you find with an error." "Once burned forever learned" is a motto that should seriously be taken to heart whenever trying to get a software reuse program started.

Speaking from personal experience at IBM, the first batch of reusable components [LSW87], which were introduced in 1987, have yet to be shown to have a defect (and in case you think that is because no one is using them— *buzzzzzz*, you're wrong; they have had hundreds of uses).

SOAPBOX: GET RID OF ALL PROGRAMMERS

Of late I have been telling people that we should take all the "programmers" and put them in a bus and push it off a cliff (much the same as should be done with "lawyers"—or so I have been told in a joke or two). But now I see the error in my ways and would like to apologize to any programmers that I may have offended. (But what they say still goes for lawyers.[1]) The point I am trying to get across when I make this outrageous statement is that programming is only part of the software problem. As professionals, we are really *problem solvers*. Given the right set of application domain-specific tools, we should be able to create solutions rapidly and reliably. I believe having the right set of reusable components goes a long way toward promoting this paradigm and that university computer science curriculum should contain at least one course in problem solving,[2] for example, *How to Solve It* [Pol73] (not to mention a course project dealing with reuse—of course).

---

[1] I suppose I should apologize to lawyers also. But my brother is a lawyer and he has convinced me that most lawyers do know how to take a joke, so never mind.

[2] Actually, there is an ongoing debate over whether or not to teach programming to students [Sol93], which addresses some of the same issues I have raised.

Finally, as pointed out by one of the reviewers of an early draft of this book, programming is how reusable parts are created in the first place. So getting rid of all the programmers means that there would be no one left to create the parts that could be used to solve the problems. Since we need someone to prime this pump, I guess a mini-van is what I should have proposed to use to drive off the cliff. That way there will be a few programmers left to create the parts and the tools/environment necessary to use them. (That also would leave room on the bus for more lawyers! :-)

SOAPBOX: REUSABLE SOFTWARE IS A CASE TOOL

As alluded to in my previous trip to the soapbox, I feel that reusable software components are tools. While most CASE (computer-aided software engineering) tools help you do work faster (and more reliably, therefore avoiding rework), software reuse eliminates work all together.[3] That is, in the case of true black box reuse, the user eliminates the cost in time and effort of test, design, and documentation (though an integration test must still be accounted for).

Postscript.   Bong! Who turned on the lights? Did you hear about the guy who stayed up all night wondering where the sun went—until it finally dawned on him? I feel this article was a turning point in my appreciation for the duality between reusing "black boxes" and reusing "patterns." If you have components to reuse, then you need to glue them together. If you have patterns to reuse, then you have the glue into which you have to stick pieces. After you glue pieces together long enough, you start seeing a pattern, then you can reuse the glue too.

I am not trying to come unglued in worrying about whether or not you get the point. Furthermore, one may think that it is easy to gather up a bunch of software components and put them in a library so people can reuse them. (The software depository approach: "Build it and they will come." Myth.) In practice, this has not worked. Software components have to be glued together and unless they were designed to be integrated (glued together easily), the integration process often outweighs the cost of writing from scratch [Big91].

---

[3] An insight pointed out to me by Barry Boehm at an ARPA SISTO meeting in Washington, D.C., in June 1991.

I think John Hughes summed it up best when he said

One can appreciate the importance of glue by an analogy with carpentry. A chair can be made quite easily by making parts—seat, legs, back and so on—and sticking them together in the right way. But this depends on the ability to make joints and wood-glue. Lacking that ability, the only way to make a chair is to carve it in one piece out of a solid block of wood.

—John Hughes [Hug89]

Chapter 6

My Personal Profiles of Programmer Personnel

PROGRAMMERS SPAN a wide range of attitudes, abilities, experience, and education. Their backgrounds influence their perception and reception of new ideas and tools. The material that follows proposes a scientific scheme for classifying programmer personnel. It is based on my personal, "opunminded" observations (and years of frustration) from dealing with software users and developers. The recognition of the programmer class or category to which these individuals belong can prove useful in developing tools and documentation, as well as in communicating with them in general.

PROGRAMMER CLASSIFICATIONS

Programmers generally fall—or are pushed or shoved—into one of five classes:

1. **NOVICES**—New, Overzealous, Very Inquisitive Computer Students,

2. **WIMPs**[1]—Well-Intentioned, Mediocre Programmers,

3. **PROS**—Perceivably Reliable, Omnipotent Software engineers,

4. **PRIMA DONNAs**—PeRmanently IMmutAble Software Developers Of Notorious Narcissistic Attitude, and

5. **DOPEs**—Dangerously Optimistic Programming Eccentrics.

---

[1]This classification was inspired by Bill Neugent's "Well Intentioned, but Mediocre People" category, which was discussed in "Preposterous Opinions About Computer Security," *SOGSAC Review*, Vol. 4, No. 3, Summer 1986.

(*Note*: Some programmers have no class, in which case they don't fit in anywhere. Unfortunately, it is beyond the scope of this chapter to discuss the backgrounds of my relatives.)

NOVICES

NOVICES are usually fresh out of school, starry-eyed, and easily motivated. They are very receptive to "playing with" new tools or adopting new development methodologies, because they are still in the learning mode. They have very little invested in previous techniques, and have yet to be burned by flaky software or hideous compiler bugs. They have yet to be christened into the real world and put through the school of hard knocks.

WIMPs

A majority, unfortunately, of the professional programmer community falls into this category. Battle scarred and war weary, they are leery of innovation. This group really needs to be sold on the technical merits of any new system or technique (that is, they need to be told what's in it for them). They are comfortable and reasonably productive with their old (possibly antiquated) tools and methodologies. Unless properly motivated or threatened, they will dismiss any efforts to extend their capabilities. The rhetorical question becomes "Can you teach an old programmer new tricks?"

PROS

These are the technical gurus in any software organization—the people to whom the NOVICES and WIMPs (but not the PRIMA DONNAs) go for assistance. "Working smarter, not harder" is their motto, and they are always receptive to using or abusing any new tool or software system that they can buy, borrow, or steal. PROS do not need to be motivated, since they will rapidly latch onto any technology that they perceive as offering them leverage and enhancing their ability to perform their jobs.

PRIMA DONNAs

PRIMA DONNAs embody the antithesis of egoless programming. They refuse to accept any new tool or technology unless they can get credit for thinking of it themselves. (After all, they are legends in their own minds.) Also, PRIMA DONNAs often lose touch with reality and develop systems that are either incomplete or totally useless to anyone but themselves. Motivating PRIMA DONNAs to step down from their thrones is a management challenge that often boils down to a battle of wills (that is, "You will do it, or else!").

DOPEs

In the broad spectrum of programmer personnel, there appears to be an over-abundance of DOPEs. Their presence is poignantly evident in the field of software reuse, where it is painfully obvious that programmers do not know how to estimate the savings in reusing a piece of software let alone how long it will take to develop and test a piece of software from scratch [WES87].

Postscript. Enabling people to make the transition from one software technology to another involves developing new tools, techniques, and associated training methods to facilitate the dissemination, assimilation, and eventual application of advances in the state of the art. The effectiveness of any approach is further enhanced when the backgrounds of the targeted individuals are taken into consideration, and the respective tools, techniques, and training methods are tailored accordingly. The classification scheme for programmer personnel proposed here addresses these issues in a pungent but pragmatic perspective.

BACKGROUND

This was fun. While not a true confession, it still uses humor to make a point about technology transfer. What is interesting to note is that I have watched myself go through each of these stages throughout my professional career. I hate to wimp out, but it is easy for one to get knocked out of the "pro" rank given the way technology is advancing so rapidly. Maybe it's time for the prima donnas to take a look at what toys the novices have been playing with. It's a whole new ballgame folks, and it looks like the rules to the game are still changing.

Finally, I should point out that the first version of this confession featured only four types of programmers. As a result of the feedback from the initial paper on programmer personnel, I have found one new category to be especially worthwhile of incorporation into the initial classification scheme. The

DOPEs classification was suggested by somebody in Poughkeepsie, whose name has been written on some misplaced piece of paper. I apologize for not being able to give credit where credit is due. If you are the person, or know the person, please contact me (just call directory assistance), and I will send you an autographed copy of this book (or a gift certificate to your favorite restaurant).[2]

---

[2] Three guesses what the choice will be.

Chapter 7

Excuses

HAVE YOU ever reached the point of frustration when you just want to scream? Well, the used program business has had its ups and downs, and lately I've been in a slump. Since I opened my new Parts Department, I have been running into all kinds of problems convincing my old customers to take advantage of these reusable components. My customers always seem to find excuses[1] for buying a new program instead of investing in some of my well-used or refurbished parts. I swear that I've heard every excuse in the book; in fact, I've decided to write them down along with translations of what I think each customer is really saying. The following, then, are the most popular excuses for not reusing software:

1. Only wimps use someone else's software.

   Translation: If I were to reuse someone else's software, then I'd be admitting that I couldn't write software myself.

2. Reuse of software destroys the ability to create it.

   Translation: It's more fun to do it myself.

3. Introduction of reusable software will eliminate my job.

   Translation: As long as I am measured by how many lines of code I write, why should I do something that reduces my perceived productivity?

4. Reusable software cannot be efficient.

   Translation: Why should I pay for all the additional baggage that someone else puts in to check software for error conditions and to add extra parameters that I'll never use? Besides, I know a better algorithm anyway.

---

[1] I thank Ed Berard of EVB Software Engineering for sharing some of his favorite excuses with me.

5. I don't want to be the first.

   Translation: Let someone else work out the bugs and pay the start-up cost to create the parts initially.

6. Trying to reuse someone else's software is a waste of my time.

   Translation: Why should I pay for some else's mistakes? The software probably has bugs in it, probably isn't very well documented, and probably won't work for my application. I'll probably spend more time trying to figure out what it does—whether or not it works—and how to modify it than I would writing it myself in the first place.

7. I don't believe that software reusability is a viable concept.

   Translation: I am too comfortable developing software the way I've been developing it for the last *n* years. Besides, I've already learned structured programming; isn't that enough?

There are many technical issues associated with making software reuse feasible. Those most often cited include determining what should be reused, how to design for reuse, how to design with reused software, and how to classify, store, and retrieve software components for reuse. However, the bottom line, I have found, is that the most prevalent excuses for not reusing software are nontechnical; they are sociological, psychological, or administrative. What we are faced with is an inherent distrust of another person's software. (What does that say about the general reputation of software quality?)

I often wonder what it will take for us to learn that if we can't do it right the first time, we can always do it over and over . . . and so the story continues.

BACKGROUND

After reading this, your mind should be filled with those clever sayings you heard as a child. For example:

"You can lead a horse to water, but you can't make it drink."

or

"Before you can reuse software, there needs to be software to reuse." [Tra88c]

There are two forces at play here. The first is getting people to reuse software, the second is getting software for people to reuse.

I believe that the only way to successfully institutionalize reuse is to *WIFM*, that is, to show all parties "What's In it For Me" and create a "win–win" situation. Management has to be able to see a return on their investment. Workers have to have something to leverage and know that they are not going to be measured in such a way that reuse will hurt their productivity. In other words, if they write less code and reuse more, their productivity should not be perceived by management as decreasing.

In my opinion, reuse is hard because it is a "double jump" (using a term coined by Marshall McLuhan, the Canadian futurist, explaining why certain technologies are revolutionary not evolutionary). Software reuse requires

1. software to reuse and

2. a process that focuses on opportunities to create reusable software and leverage existing resources.

Unless both are in place, reuse will not "just happen."

SOAPBOX: PAY NOW OR PAY LATER

Reuse is a long-term investment, plain and simple. There is a saying that one of my former managers, Bob Barnes, pounded into my head:

> *"Why is there always enough money to do it over, but never enough money to do it right the first time?"*

For a long time, this was the case, but not so today. Interestingly enough, my current manager, Rodger Fritz, has a three by four foot banner adorning his office wall stating:

> *"Do it right the first time!"*

I take this as a sign of encouragement and support for software reuse. I know that I am not alone in having this opinion. Tom DeMarco at the 13th International Conference on Software Engineering in Austin, Texas, 1991, stated that

"Reuse is a management issue."

To reinforce this thought, Masao Matsumoto from NEC, at the same conference made, what I feel, is a painfully accurate observation of the U.S. software industry:

"The difference between Japanese and U.S. software industry is that we look at software reuse as a long-term investment."

So, there are many excuses for not "doing reuse" and current public opinion has it earmarked as a management problem.

PERCEPTION

Chapter 8

Reusability Comes of Age

FOR YEARS, I have used an analogy that compares used cars to used programs. I think this analogy holds for pungent and pragmatic reasons: People are leery about buying a used car for many of the same reasons programmers are reluctant to reuse someone else's work. With this analogy in mind, I offer some of my own insights—as a seasoned veteran of many used program sales—into the problems of software reuse and what factors have inhibited its acceptance as a viable form of software development.

NEW OR USED?

Before deciding on whether to invest in a new or used car, a prospective buyer should first identify his or her needs (features, performance, price range). Other factors, like urgency, may constrain the selection process to a vehicle on the lot instead of one ordered from the factory. In any case, the buyer should develop a strategy for evaluating candidates.

The next step is to shop around. Will a potential candidate that looks good on paper really live up to everything a smooth-talking salesperson says?

STANDARD FEATURES

The first question that needs to be answered is "Does the vehicle meet the customer's requirements?" Some models have options (a convertible roof, four-wheel drive) that enhance their adaptability to future operating environments. But these features may just be extra baggage that interferes with overall performance or adds to maintenance costs.

Clearly, if a software program meets the customer's basic requirements, then it warrants further consideration. But program options are mixed blessings: On one hand, parameters aid adaptation of the software to future needs;

on the other hand, they can result in normal operating inefficiencies and increased maintenance costs.

MILEAGE

A new or low-mileage used car, in all probability, will require less maintenance than a high-mileage used car. Yet finding a low-mileage car on a used car lot is cause for suspicion, since most people would not part with it unless it was giving them problems. But software is unfatiguing, so the higher the mileage (the more users, the more systems it is available on, or the longer it has been in use) the more desirable it is. History has proven that the number of bugs found in software decreases with use, assuming other factors remain the same.

MAINTENANCE RECORD

Knowing the types of repairs made on a vehicle and the quality of the maintenance effort will influence a customer's decision. If serious problems occurred early in the vehicle's life but were properly repaired, they will not weigh as heavily in the selection process.

A customer can readily evaluate the quality of a program by looking at the type, severity, and date of problems found in a piece of software. If many miles have been put on the program since the last change or if the types of updates have been insignificant, the prospective buyer can place more confidence in the product. The customer should avoid a situation where the maintenance record indicates that more problems are introduced each time one problem is fixed.

REPUTATION

If no maintenance record is available, the customer can estimate the reliability of the vehicle by associating it with the overall quality of the manufacturer's vehicles.

Similarly, if a software manufacturer has a track record of delivering quality programs, the customer can place more trust in other programs that manufacturer sells.

APPEARANCE

Kicking the tires and checking the paint job and trim are other ways the customer can gain useful information. Sometimes it pays to have a skilled mechanic perform a close inspection under the hood to determine potential problem areas (temporary repairs or shoddy workmanship).

A software buyer can also tell shoddy workmanship by examining the exterior (the user interface and documentation) of a program. Looking under the hood helps the customer assess certain programming characteristics (naming and commenting conventions) that can indicate the overall maintainability, modifiability, and reliability of the component or product.

STANDARDS

Standard instrumentation and compliance to safety and operating standards (seat belts and emission control) give customers a feeling of confidence in the product. Standard compliance dispels some of the fears of being stuck with a lemon.

If a piece of software complies with certain standards (in documentation, interface design, and testing), its potential for reuse is increased because of the perceived quality and usability of the software.

WARRANTY

What happens if something goes wrong? Will the dealer fix the problem or will the customer be left holding the bag/bug?

To establish the credibility and viability of new and used programs and components, the seller should provide both a policy for determining responsibility for error and a mechanism for resolving problems.

If a program does not meet all of the customer's requirements, the manufacturer, dealer, or customer is faced with the task of modification. What options are available, and how easily is a program customized? These characteristics play an important role in determining the overall reusability of a program. Finally, the buyer should ask how customization affects the warranty. If things go wrong, the new owner might have difficulty soliciting assistance from the original manufacturer if the program has since been modified.

OPTIONS

Because customer requirements and tastes vary, a manufacturer provides options to satisfy the customer's needs as closely as possible. Certain options must be installed by the manufacturer; others can be installed by factory-trained mechanics; still others can be installed by the customer. In any case, the risk associated with adding an option decreases as the expertise of the person making the changes increases.

ACCESSIBILITY

Customers don't want to waste their time driving all around town to find the car that meets their needs. Dealers who advertise a large selection have a better chance of attracting business.

Similarly, the convenience of shopping or getting a program serviced locally is very appealing. The less effort customers have to expend in finding candidates for reuse the more likely they are to buy them.

PRICE

When buying a new or used car off the lot customers have to pay for whatever options come with the car, whether or not they were on the customer's original list of options.

Programs require investments in both capital and time. Off-the-shelf software is often sold as a package deal. In this case, the customer may be paying for more functions than required and will end up dragging around extra options that they neither need nor have space for.

Similarly, the customer has to pay the price for learning how to drive the new software effectively and how to maintain it. These hidden prices, plus the price of failure, must be factored into the buy-or-build decision.

TEST DRIVE

The acid test to determine the suitability of a candidate is the test drive. The buyer can experience the true feel for how a car handles under different driving conditions and can project realistically what it would be like to own.

A customer who tries a program on for size can determine if any rough spots exist in the user interface and how the program performs under simulated working conditions (if possible). If the problems are minor, the seller might be able to customize the software before consummating the sale.

INTANGIBLE INHIBITORS

The reputation of used car salesmen and the products they promote is somewhat negative. Getting stuck with a lemon is a major concern of most used car customers. This same lack of trust in programming products has been the major inhibitor in advancing software reuse. Unfortunately, because it is often easier to write an incorrect program than to understand a correct program, programmer productivity (which would increase if software developers didn't reinvent the wheel each time) and program quality (which would increase if they used high-quality parts) have not evolved.

Two other reasons may explain why the used program market originally envisioned by M. D. McIlroy [McI69] in 1968 has failed to materialize:

1. There are no clearly defined standards, either for developing reusable software or for systems based on reusable software.

2. There are neither large repositories of reusable software and components nor the tools to access and synthesize systems from them.

What will it take to create a successful used program business?

- *Quality parts*: Customers should have confidence that what they buy will perform without error.

- *Standard interfaces*: Customers should be able to use what they buy in a manner that complies with standard operating conventions. Software should be easily integrated into new or existing systems.

- *Documentation*: Customers should understand what the software they buy does, how they can use it, and how they can modify it if necessary.

- *Selection*: Customers should have a choice of options available on what they buy.

Nothing is better than cruising along in a high-performance, well-tuned program with complete confidence in the safety of all those who depend on you to get the job done. Unfortunately, the state of the practice today has us lumbering along in a clunker that spends most of its time in the shop undergoing repairs and has the distinct possibility of crashing due to some unforeseen manufacturing defect.

BACKGROUND

This piece appeared as the guest editor's introduction to a special issue of *IEEE Software* on "Software Reuse" in 1987. While I held back on the satire, the analogy is still compelling—and a fun one to make. The sad reality is that, eight years later, the "reuse" silver bullet is still being loaded into the chamber, only to misfire. The problem is that people don't know what they are aiming at, or don't have enough powder to make the kill. You will be able to read more about this "silver bullet" in Chapter 15.

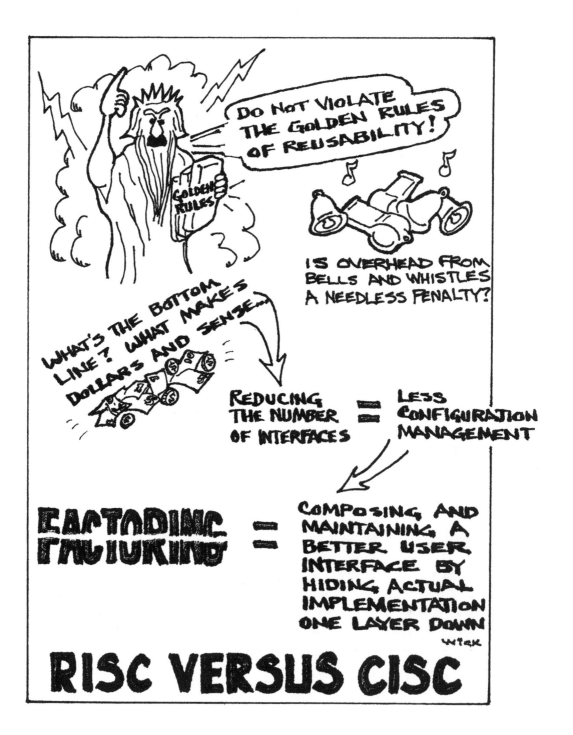

Chapter 9

The RISC Versus CISC Debate

J̲UST WHEN things seemed to be going smoothly, a battle of epic proportions started brewing down at the used program shop. I never thought we would have a RISC versus CISC debate[1] related to used programs, but as I always say, "If the module has the right parameters, call it." And that really was the crux of the problem. You see, my customers seemed to have gotten a bad case of the WIBNIs (the "Wouldn't It Be Nice Ifs"[2]). My programmers, eager to please existing customers and attract new ones, started adding new parameters and options to existing software packages and building blocks. At first, this tactic gave the desired results: it increased each module's "domain of applicability" [PD87], thereby increasing its reuse. But pretty soon the advantages of having all these options actually decreased a program's reusability because customers grew unable to comprehend the dependencies and interactions between the options. We had violated two of the Golden Rules of Reusability: (1) Before you can reuse something, you have to know what it does; and (2) before you can reuse something, you have to know how to reuse it.[3]

Furthermore, the customers were concerned about dragging around all the extra code for the options they didn't use, thus paying for the additional size and functions they didn't want or need. More importantly, I realized that these multifaceted, monolithic modules were becoming harder to document and maintain.

---

[1] *Note*: One of the original Reduced Instruction Set Computer (RISC) versus Complex Instruction Set Computer (CISC) debates took place in Palo Alto, California, at the Fifteenth Annual Workshop on Microprogramming, Oct. 5–7, 1982, between Mike Flynn of Stanford University, Nick Tredennick, then at IBM and formerly of Motorola, and David Patterson of UC Berkeley and John Hennesy of Stanford.

[2] I first encountered this term in Peter Brown's *Starting with Unix* (Addison-Wesley Publishing Company, 1984).

[3] The first Golden Rule of Reusability is "Before you can reuse something, you have to find it."

This is how the great RISC (Reduced Interface Software Component) versus CISC (Complex Interface Software Component) debate began. Should software subroutines have complex or simple interfaces? The CISC proponents wanted to throw everything, including the kitchen sink, through the one interface, arguing that with intelligent defaults their interfaces were as simple to use as the RISC interfaces. The RISC side pointed out that the overhead from dragging around all of the extra logic to handle the bells and whistles (which were seldom used anyway) was a needless penalty for the most frequently used operations. They argued that the CISC format could be replaced by a series of RISC operations. The CISC camp countered by pointing out that to achieve the same power as a CISC operation, a RISC implementation would result in more context switches (notorious cycle burners). They observed that, although their operations were slightly slower than the RISC subroutines, they could do more at once because they had more opportunities for parallelism. The RISC side countered that their interface allowed the same parallelism with more flexibility and better user control. The CISC side scored their biggest points when they argued that the RISC approach would fail in a multitasking situation, where multiple threads of control could adversely affect each other through side effects.

Somehow, as I watched this debate, I had the feeling of *déjà vu*. Personally, I was most interested in the bottom line—what made dollars and sense. I preferred reducing the number of interfaces because that would result in less configuration management, and I knew that current optimization technology could take care of the dead code problem.

The conclusion that I came to was that both camps had some valuable points to make. The RISC people were right when they said that the CISC people were not exercising caution in their application of "tail-fin" technology. Instead of increasing the domain of applicability, we were approaching the domain of absurdity. The CISC people were right in trying to provide additional function, but they had missed the opportunity to practice what they preach (modularization). One of the fundamental underlying software principles of reusable software development is factoring: developing a hierarchy of reusable components (each capable of performing a single function) and combining these reusable components through inheritance, instantiation, or simple importation. Factoring breaks a monolithic module into pieces. This practice helps the programmer to compose and maintain a better user interface by hiding the actual implementation one layer down.

We learn by our mistakes, but I wish we didn't have to relearn things so often.

BACKGROUND

To understand why I enjoyed chewing on this piece so much before I spit it out, there are a few things that you need to know about my background. From my first confessions, you may recall that I am a bit twiddler from way back— a microprogrammer[4] tried and true. I was chairman of the ACM Special Interest Group in Microprogramming for three years (1989–1992), and before that, their newsletter editor for 5 years (1983–1988). I was the chair of the 15th Annual Workshop on Microprogramming when the RISC versus CISC debate was in its highest hype. It is with great relish that I carried this parody over to software. It is with greater relish that I see the RISC instruction set getting CISC-ier—but that is a topic for discussion in front of a different audience.

---

[4] Microprogramming is an alternative form of designing and implementing the control logic of a digital device [Tra82]—not programming microprocessors!

Chapter 10

Programming-in-the-New

O K, IT'S time to fall on my sword again. Another revelation has just hit me right where it hurts the most—in the wallet. Having gone through the "old school" of programming (assembly language, FORTRAN, COBOL, and PL/I), I consider myself an experienced, battle-scarred veteran of many programming wars. But, as the result of an opportunity I couldn't refuse, I have spent the last years retooling at the "new school" of software engineering (Ada, Prolog, and Smalltalk). Now I consider myself a somewhat naive, battle-scared beginner thrust into the front line of new softwars.

Regarding my business of developing and selling reusable programs, I have come to the realization that it is time to switch horses; that my programming-in-the-old mind-set has reached its limits of productivity and profitability, and it is time to harness the new (to me) technology and adopt new programming paradigms to the business at hand.

REUSE AND PROGRAMMING-IN-THE-OLD

As I reminisce about the good old days, I begin to realize that they were the "old days" and that there wasn't really that much "good" about them (other than the fact that my ego was bigger and there was more hair on the top of my head). When people talk about growing pains, the birth of the programming profession gave a new meaning to the word labor. Key punches, and waiting three to four hours for a batch job to turn around (only to find you missed a comma in your JCL), hardly bring back sweet memories. We did the best we could with the coding forms and "flaw charts"[1] we had for tools. The field was young, and we were having too much fun to know any better. Besides, we were becoming legends in our own minds—who could argue with success?

---

[1] I first encountered this term in David Gries' *The Science of Programming* [Gri89].

FORTRAN subroutine and assembler language macro libraries were the primary technologies we had to ply our trade of reusable software. APL and LISP function libraries had some cute features (e.g., iterators, maps, and just being interpretive) that never really seemed to catch on with most mainframe macho machine-code mainliners. Functional decomposition worked well—most of the time. The only problem with top-down stepwise refinement was that in the used programming business we needed to work bottom-up to capitalize on our library of subroutines and macros. Working top-down and bottom-up, we sometimes didn't meet in the middle—a somewhat annoying situation. Also, adding more parameters and writing larger macros (later called *application generators*) only scaled so far until they collapsed under their own complexity. I felt that the used program business was not evolving, and lacked an adequate technical foundation on which to build.

PROGRAMMING-IN-THE-NEW

Has there been a revolution in the used programming business, or has software technology just taken the path of least resistance, with the law of the bungle determining the survival of the witless? In my case, I certainly was skeptical that artificial intelligence (AI) would ever provide anything to make my job easier. All the hype that I read about expert systems sent me quickly searching for the "del" key. But, upon further examination, I found several really clever ideas lurking in the myths.

Formal methods helped me assert the correctness of my reusable components as well as verify their interfaces. Language features such as user-defined types were abstract at first, but along with certain parameterization capabilities, they were just the type of thing I was looking for. Data abstraction and encapsulation along with information hiding became the basis for developing a collection of reusable components. Finally, programming by difference using hierarchies of types helped localize the common operations and distinguish the unique characteristic of my reusable software.

After wrestling with several new software development methodologies, I realized that an object-oriented approach suited my top-down and bottom-up design style. Using a layered approach, I seldom ran into the problem of designs not meeting in the middle. I have always believed that what sets reusable software apart is how it is put together. These new technologies helped me take systems apart and put them back together more easily and with less expense in time and money.

The expert system engineers had provided insight into one tough reuse problem that remained: How does one reuse software artifacts other than just code? In their search for storing knowledge, the AI researchers had tried various representation methods, which along with the sophisticated graphical programming environment provided the missing link in my reuse environment. Now I could capture the design decisions along with the design for future reuse using a hypertext system. Furthermore, I could track which of my requirements were satisfied by what part of my design and implemented in what part of my code. If my requirements changed, I could quickly find out where the code needed to be changed. There was even some talk about parameterizing the requirements so the changes would automatically filter down to the implementation.

I still wasn't done recycling and adapting expert system technology to program reuse; all the domain analysis techniques easily transferred to identifying and parameterizing new systems.

Time and technology wait for no one, and technical obsolescence can rapidly reduce one's ability to compete in the marketplace. I have switched so I can fight for my market share. Most of the software technologies that I identified in the previous section have been around at least 10 to 15 years (object-oriented programming was introduced in 1960). It has just taken this long for the price per MIPS (million instructions per second) to decrease enough to make the technology attractive for widespread reuse. The bottom line is that it makes cents—dollars and cents—to leverage the new technology.

BACKGROUND

This is a scary revelation as I reflect on it now. I wonder how many people can relate to it? What scares me is the realization that so much has happened in the last five years since I wrote this piece. While this article focuses mostly on language issues, keeping on top of graphical user interfaces and multimedia workstation technology is providing the biggest challenge for us old-timers (and a few new-timers too, I imagine)!

In the words of Bob Dylan, "The times they are a changing." In fact, if this were five years from now, I suspect you would be reading this at your hand-held wireless multimedia workstation, or listening to it being read to you, if that's what you wanted.

Chapter 11

Reuseless Software

HAVE YOU ever tripped down the primrose path of least resistance, commending yourself for building a new program by salvaging someone else's software, only to be startled by the harsh reality that things were not as great as you had planned?

True, you thought you were building on someone else's successes, but you had not counted on inheriting their mistakes or finding out, too late, that what you thought you could reuse "as is" required a lot more effort than you had planned. The software you were trying to salvage might be good, but for what? You budgeted time and staff to salvage or carry over code from the last project, only to find that it didn't work as advertised, if the fact that it worked was advertised at all.

Ignoring blatant errors of commission, the subtle errors of omission are the ones that really require the most effort to overcome (e.g., failure to document implementation decisions or failure to test for certain pathological conditions). The software might work well in the narrow context for which it was designed, but taken out of its specific domain the software suddenly becomes brittle—in other words, reuseless. For example, you might want to reuse one of the dozen or so linked-list packages lying around your project, but, wouldn't you know it, the one you pick has only four of the five operations you need. The missing operation is in another package, but that one happens to be missing one of the other operations you desire.

So, what do you do? What do you want to do? Modify one, modify both, or start from scratch?

A good used program salesman does not often suggest starting over, but adapting or extending someone else's software can be a programmer's nightmare. Reuseless code is software that is not worth reengineering for a new application. Any programmer can find it challenging, to say the least, to track down global references, operating system and hardware dependencies, or subtle coding tricks that only make sense (if at all) to the original implementor (even though you could swear that no one in his or her right mind would ever write such code).

Sometimes, programmers should let old code die a natural death rather than spend any effort trying to revive it. As many of us have learned from experience, plenty of reuseless code is lying around (one might argue that a lot of it was useless code in the first place). Not that most code is reuseless (or more important, needs to be created as reuseless), but software not specifically designed to be reused is simply more difficult and costly to reuse. Similarly, code designed for reuse (reuseful code) might cost 30% to 200% more to develop, document, and test, but subsequent reuse costs 20% to 40% less than rewriting.

Making software reusable exacts a cost in experience and effort. Creating reusable robust interfaces requires insight in seeing how software has been used in the past and envisioning how it might be used in the future. Furthermore, because the most important quality of reusable software is that it be quality software, emphasis should be placed on thoroughly specifying, testing, and certifying that the software has achieved a certain level of operational and documentation quality. Only then will programmers be willing to invest their time to consider its reuse. (Or, as I like to say, only then will business be back to reusual.)

The choice is simple: You can pay for it now, or pay for it again later. However, having experienced the joy of good plagiaristic programming, one might agree with the words of a colleague of mine, Ev Merritt: "We need to give the acronym NIH[1] back to the National Institutes of Health."

BACKGROUND

What can I say? What you have read is true. In the years that have passed since I wrote this piece, several CASE tool manufacturers have lined their pockets by selling reengineering elixirs. I am not saying they aren't good tools. What I am saying is that they are not a panacea for finding/"mining" reusable software components. There is still a dearth of "domain analysis" tools, although several domain analysis processes are emerging [KCH+90, PD91b], including the one I have been responsible for developing [TC92] that is found in Appendix A.

---

[1] The acronym "NIH" is usually associated with the phrase "Not Invented Here."

SOAPBOX: COST OF REUSE

I have developed a cost model for determining the cost of developing "reusable" software. This model appears in software Myth #8 in Chapter 17. Obviously, costs vary based on the domain being addressed (he says hedgingly). What the model does is to point out areas where intellectual effort needs to be spent. There is an up-front cost for developing reusable software that amounts to from 25% to 100% depending on the degree to which it is parameterized, documented, and verified.

Chapter 12

The Same Old Song

WHEN YOU are in the software reuse business you become proficient at recognizing patterns. Here is a pattern that really struck a familiar chord.

I can't help but note that many of my most successful used program salesmen have been musicians[1] at one time in their illustrious careers. They are perfectionists at mastering their instruments. Whether working on a piece of software or playing a piece of music, they are outstanding performers. When their fingers hit the keyboard, what comes out is magic.

As a well-schooled musician myself, I am convinced there is an uncanny parallel between the skills necessary for second-hand software sales and service and those required for musical scales and performance.

- Music is a codification of a sequence of directions on what should be played. It contains certain parameters that control variations in tempo and volume.

- Software is a codification of a sequence of directions on what should be performed. Programs have certain parameters that control the selection of variations in speed and storage. (This is especially true of the used programs I sell.)

- Music is organized into a series of movements.

- Programs are organized into a collection of modules.

- Musicians often learn several different instruments.

- Programmers often learn several different languages.

---

[1] It would be unfair for me to say that this is a requirement. Some of the best programmers I know can only play a stereo!

- Musicians learn patterns. They learn chords, inversions, progressions, riffs, and turnarounds. Furthermore, they learn to transpose these patterns into a different key or adapt the music to different rhythms.

- Programmers learn instruction sequences and algorithms. They learn to apply them to different kinds of data and data structures or adapt them to different environments.

- Beginning musicians learn classic standard arrangements written by masters.

- Beginning programmers learn classic standard algorithms written by masters.

- Most professional musicians learn composition and orchestration.

- Most professional specialists in second-hand software learn composition and generation.

- Serious musicians must learn music theory.

- Serious programmers must learn automata theory, the theory of computational complexity, and the like.

- Musicians have to spend long hours practicing to reach perfection in a piece of music.

- Programmers (often) have to spend long hours trying to reach perfection in a piece of software. (In my humble opinion, this effort is often a waste of creative talent. When programmers construct new software systems from well-tested reusable software components, they spend less time and effort developing a higher quality system.)

- Most experienced musicians can play back an entire musical arrangement inside their heads.

- Most experienced programmers can play back the entire logic structure of a program inside their heads.

- Musicians work together to produce a concert of complex sounds. They listen to each other and try to complement each other's work when playing in a group.

- Programmers strive to work in harmony to produce complex applications. Specialists in second-hand software listen to the customer's needs and adapt their programs accordingly as well as complement the work of their fellow programmers.

Reusable software developers, like musicians, exhibit an artistic flair. They have that blend of inspiration, perspiration, and dedication that sings success. Most importantly, as artists, they can appreciate the work of others. They show no hesitation incorporating other programmers' works into their own personal repertoire.

Mark Twain once spoke of a musician who wrote music that was better than it sounded. I know of several programmers who have written programs that were better than they sounded (and programs that, unfortunately, sounded better than they were).

So, let me offer a bit of sound advice to potential used program suppliers and consumers. Even though I don't keep score, every time someone reuses one of my programs, it's music to my ears. Play it again, Sam.

BACKGROUND

This piece, by far, generated the most feedback (both pro and con) of anything I had published in *IEEE Computer*. When I wrote it I had no idea that it might offend anyone. But, as you probably have noticed by now, I am clearly marching to the beat of a different drummer (or maybe I am not playing with a full deck, or worse yet, tone deaf). On that note, I will end.

Chapter 13

IPLing the System

ALL IS not well in reuse land. It seems that while the elves were all busy at their workstations, cutting and pasting pieces of reusable software together, some grinch snuck in and IPLed[1] the system. The results were disastrous; the reuse libraries were scrubbed clean. Nothing was spared from this massive purge. Not only were the programmers stripped of the tools of their trade (source code to hack), but most of the documentation was gone too. Worst of all, some of the programmers were found to be contaminated and had to be put in quarantine! (The doctor says they'll be OK in a couple of years if they stay away from the kind of software that caused the problem.) Just when I thought things couldn't get any worse, someone came up and told me that I couldn't sell and reuse a program that I designed and wrote two years ago (after extensively surveying the literature, I must add) because someone else had the idea three years ago, and just got around to publishing it today. I wanted to cry foul, but all I could do was cry, once I knew what I was up against. It was a frightening experience that has left me paranoid and a bit more conservative in my ways.

Does this sound far-fetched? Have I been hitting the bit bucket a little too hard lately? I only wish that were true. Unfortunately, this is an all too real scenario. In my case, IPL does not stand for "initial program load," as us old bit twiddlers learned, but "intellectual property law," and the grinch that stole the used programs is an IPL lawyer armed with an injunction. This scenario is quite relevant to software reuse, especially when the software comes from unknown sources. There is an old saying about "assuming" something to be true. In this case, one can get into a lot of trouble by assuming that a piece of software is in the public domain. One really needs to be careful in establishing how a piece of software came into being or else one can be in for a big surprise.

---

[1] *Note*: The term "IPL" in the programming domain has traditionally been associated with the operation "initial program load," a bootstrap operation normally associated with starting up a system.

There is an old saying about "getting what you pay for" and that "the best things in life are free." Well, in this case, I believe "if you see it lying on the street, don't pick it up" is much more appropriate.

Reusing software verbatim requires making a copy. Copying software is not always legal, as most everyone knows. A problem occurs when someone modifies or reuses part or all of a version of someone else's software, or even uses the design as a basis for new software.[2] In either case, the software can be viewed as a work derived from the original, hence all rights to the preexisting work belong to the original creator—except what was added. Also, translating software from one language to another can be considered creating a derivative work, therefore, it is also illegal (assuming one did not get authorization to do so or write it from scratch in the first place). Things get worse. For instance, creating a plug-compatible piece of software without even looking at someone else's code (using a black box approach) has even been the cause for litigation. Unfortunately, merely looking at someone else's source code (whether you have it, or decompile it; whether you think it is in the public domain or not) may reveal something that later turns out to be a trade secret, in which case you run the risk of being excluded from developing similar applications for a period of time in the future. Finally, there is the whole issue of software patents, where you can do a patent search, then in good faith develop some software that a year or two later turns out to infringe on a patent that some-one had filed before your search, but that wasn't issued (and revealed) until later.

Yes, we are living in interesting times. I often wonder if there are more lawyers than programmers? I'll tell you one thing for sure, I am all for intellec-tual property rights, but now that I know more about them, I have become extremely cautious. Once, I never used to look at a gift piece of reusable soft-ware in the mouth. Now, I really check its pedigree.

BACKGROUND

I owe the inspiration for this piece to a lovely winter I spent in Philadelphia during the summer of 1990. I shouldn't make fun of the city of brotherly love, but what I was doing there had nothing to do with that aspect of human relationships. I was in Philadelphia to participate in a follow-up to a federal

---

[2] At the time of this writing, the reuse of design was argumentatively considered copyright infringe-ment, based on [Whe87], but recent court decisions [Sam90, Sam92] have reversed this ruling.

antitrust suit. It was related to microcode, which I knew a lot about, and copyright, which, due to opportunities that had presented themselves as a member of the IBM Corporate Reuse Council's Reuse Technology Steering Committee, I also knew a lot about. Being involved in a trial of such magnitude was a truly unique experience. Staying in five-star hotels somewhat offset the 14- to 16-hour days spent preparing for depositions and analyzing testimony[3] and "evidence." I must say that the degree of professionalism, attention to detail, thoroughness in preparation, and intensity that the trial lawyers displayed were unique. I wish more programmers had that sense of commitment to detail. I also wish more programmers got paid the six-figure salaries these lawyers commanded—only if they deserved it, of course.

---

[3] Working with Fred Brook's son, who was a lawyer on the case, turned out to be another pleasant experience, since Brook's *The Mythical Man-Month* [Bro75] has been the inspiration of many in the programming profession.

Chapter 14

"Not Again!"

LATELY I have been both encouraged and discouraged by the surge of interest in used program sales and service.

Encouraged, for instance, by requests like the one from Barry Boehm, director of DARPA's Software and Intelligent Systems Technology Office. He has issued the "Megaprogramming Challenge" [Boe90] to researchers, calling on them to develop the technology for constructing software "one component at a time rather than one line of code at a time."

This adds some credibility to the used program business, which is booming. It seems like every time I turn around, a new dealership is popping up. Misery loves company, I always say. Not that being a used program salesperson isn't fun. It is, and I really do enjoy the competition. It's just that the owners of these new establishments may not really be prepared for this line of business. They don't seem to practice what they preach, and I fear they are doomed to fall into the same potholes that caused other used program dealerships to crash and burn.

In graduate school I learned that an hour in the library can save a month in the laboratory. This lesson applies also to a library of used programs that could save valuable time designing, coding, documenting, and testing new programs. But this is not the turkey I want to roast.

I want to focus on "advances" in the state of the art in software reuse. Doug McIlroy first proposed used program sales in 1968 at the NATO Conference on Software Engineering [McI69]. My suspicions on the (lack of) progress in the field since then were confirmed recently by Peter Freeman. In his keynote address to the First International Workshop on Software Reuse, July 1991, in Dortmund, Germany, Peter observed that software reuse researchers were "stepping on each other's toes, rather than standing on each other's shoulders." He suggested that instead of 23 years of progress in advancing the state of the art in software reuse, researchers had repeated 1 year of progress 23 times.

But then again, why should we be any different from anyone else? I have often heard that new technology needs to be invented three times before it catches on. I guess that in our case, we just have to reinvent it three times.

BACKGROUND

The material in this piece was inspired by a sense of *déjà vu* I had; either that or it was a bad porkchop I had for supper. To the alert reader, I suppose that I am beginning to sound like a whiner. I know, "If you aren't part of the solution, then you're probably part of the problem." And "There he goes again! Complain! Complain! Complain!" I wish I had the answer! I wish there was an answer! If anyone finds the answer, please let me know.

You can call collect.

"SILVER BULLET"

"DEPOSITORIES" FOR EXISTING SOFTWARE COMPONENTS

NEW APPLICATIONS FIRED OUT IN QUICK SUCCESSION

COUPLING SOFTWARE ARCHITECTURES WITH PROTOTYPING LANGUAGES, OBJECT MANAGERS, AND HYPERMEDIA CASE TOOLS

WICK

THE GOLDEN GUN

Chapter 15

The Golden Gun

I N THE past, does it seem that management sent you to "hunt the big prey" and it turned out that all you could do was "hunt and pray big." Some managements have decreed that reuse is a silver bullet and have established "depositories" for existing software components. There are four problems with this approach:

1. Some of this "ammunition" turns out to be a dud (the silver bullets had no powder in the casings).

2. The ammunition comes from all different places and it is hard to tell what caliber it is.

3. You have no gun to fire it out of.

4. There is no clear target to shoot.

Although it is true that "silver" bullets cost more than "regular" bullets, just as reusable software costs more than single-shot implementations, the price is worth it, if the number of targets you can shoot at increases. But, because bullets are far more effective when you have a gun (with good sights) to shoot them from, the real focus of the problem is that you need a software architecture into which you can fit reusable components. Granted this "golden gun" doesn't come cheap, but given the advantages of interoperability, adaptability, and extendability, it is well worth the price.

The increasing interest in software architectures is witnessed by Anita Jone's keynote address at ICSE 15 (1993) in Baltimore, and the tutorial on the same topic by Mary Shaw and David Garlan of Carnegie Mellon University. Furthermore, it is personally satisfying to see progress in the ARPA-funded Domain-Specific Software Architecture (DSSA) program [GM92].

Finally, I may be off target, but I envision coupling software architectures with prototyping languages, object managers, and hypermedia CASE tools to create a machine gun, where new applications can be fired in quick succession. That should mow down the competition pretty fast and go a long way toward eliminating the hand-to-hand combat we are faced with down in the trenches today.

BACKGROUND

The insight for this observation came from four years of work on the ARPA-funded DSSA program [Met90, GM92, CST92]. Although most software developers seem satisfied to reuse "code," others have been focusing on pushing reuse earlier in the software development life cycle. In addition, researchers are realizing that the "S" in DSSA stands for "system" as well as "software." That is, all of the technology, methodology, and infrastructure to support software architecture component specification, configuration, and reuse applies to hardware components also.

Chapter 16

Software Reuse Maxims

OFTENTIMES REUSE discussions mix "theology" with "technology." Many nights I have lain in bed pondering over the issues of software reuse; wondering what the answers were, or better yet, wondering what the questions were.[1] This chapter contains some of my observations on the *practice and malpractice* of software reuse. I will be reflecting on what I call *reusable software maxims*, based on my personal experience with the joys and frustrations of trying to reuse software. I will be touching on a lot of ideas that many of you are familiar with along with some concepts that might be new to you. (Some of the concepts are relatively new to me—although they have been around for quite a while, they seemed to have stopped somewhere before they got to me.)

In any case, I think these concepts are *essential* for understanding and harnessing the underlying technology that supports the development *of* reusable software and the development of new systems *with* reusable software.

GOLDEN RULES OF REUSABILITY

Before you can reuse something, you need to

1. *find it,*

2. *know what it does, and*

3. *know how to reuse it.*

The first of these "golden rules" is sort of a Catch-22. Because:

---

[1] The material in this chapter is based on my keynote address for the Spring 1988 National Symposium and Workshop on Software Reusability sponsored by the National Institute for Software Quality and Productivity, April 13–15, 1988, in Washington, D.C. Furthermore, the artwork was inspired by the reuse rabbi, Martin Griss.

Before you can reuse something, there has to be something to reuse.

The second rule implies that you are not going to reuse something if it's not going to do the job. Rephrasing this rule a bit, one could say:

Before you can reuse something, it needs to be useful.

The final rule states that before you can use or reuse software, you need to know how to invoke it, what the parameters are, or in the worst case, how to modify it so that it performs the function that you really want.

There also is a fourth unspoken golden rule of reuse. Before we (and I include myself here) will reuse something, we need to be convinced it will save us time and effort. Woodfield, Embley, and Scott at BYU [WES87] have found empirical evidence that the perceived savings has to be greater than 30% before a person attempts to reuse it.

This leads us to the next observation, which is actually Ted Biggerstaff's Reuse Rules of Three[2] [Tra88a]. Ted based them on Bob Lanergans and C. A. Grasso's observations at Raytheon [LG84].

BIGGERSTAFF'S REUSE RULES OF THREE

1. *Before you can develop reusable software you need to have developed it* three *times.*

2. *Before you can reap the benefits of reuse, you need to reuse it at least* three *times.*

What the first rule says is that domain analysis is hard. That is, before you can determine if it is worthwhile to make something reusable, you need to have some *insight* and *experience* in order to create the most reusable interface.

The second rule acknowledges the fact that software that is designed to be reused is from 30% to 200% *more expensive to build* (see Software Myth #3 in Chapter 17 for a cost breakdown). This is due in part to the increased cost of domain analysis, design, documentation, and testing.

---

[2] Ted is currently leading a component-based software composition research project at Microsoft Corporation. Prior to that he was director of a reuse project at MCC where he published extensively on the subject [Big86a, Big86b, Big87, BR87a, BR87b]. Ted has the distinction of being the chair of the first Reuse Conference in 1983 [ITT83] and has edited, with A. J. Perlis, a book on reuse published by Addison Wesley [BP89].

Finally, developing software from reusable components requires the modification of existing software development processes as well as training and guidelines.

I like the Japanese software factory approach used in the past at Hitachi [TM87]. Once a month, typically on a Friday afternoon, they required all programmers to perform a programming exercise—to write a simple program. The requirements were defined such that a straightforward solution could be constructed from the components in their reusable software library. Then on Monday morning, the members of each department evaluated the solutions for style and correctness. This process not only encouraged familiarity with the reusable software repository, but it reinforced programming guidelines for documentation and implementation style.

SOFTWARE REUSE WILL BECOME THE EXPERT SYSTEMS OF THE 1990S

These words were spoken to me by Mary Shaw of the Software Engineering Institute at Carnegie Mellon University. She was alluding to all the *hype* that has been associated with expert systems and expressing her reservations about the potential overselling of the benefits of software reuse.

Let me repeat: *"There is no free lunch when it comes to software reuse"* [Tra88a]. It is essential not to get caught up in the emotion of the moment and make broad sweeping generalizations about potential productivity improvements with reusable software. The economics of reuse vary from problem domain to problem domain and from environment to environment. Depending on the tools, languages, and methods applied, various degrees of productivity improvement can be realized.

SOFTWARE REUSE SAVINGS ACCOUNT

Software Reuse is like a savings account; before you can collect any interest, you have to make a deposit, and the more you put in, the greater the dividend.

—Ted Biggerstaff [Tra88a]

In reflecting on this maxim, it is interesting to note how small the deposit can be. In certain narrow, well-defined problem domains such as banking, insurance, or EDP, *25 to 75* useful abstractions have proven to be *all that are necessary* for building new applications. Notice that I said *abstractions, not components*. This is an important distinction that depends on the programming tools available. Furthermore, a language greatly influences a person's reuse *mind-set* and how programmers develop reusable abstractions.

Borrowing an example from Ed Berard [Ber86] of EVB Software Engineering, Inc., suppose you are asked to come up with a solution for the following problem: Design and implement a stack. If you had a *FORTRAN mind-set*, you would use an array. It is efficient and does the job. If you had a *Pascal mind-set*, you might use a linked list. It is more flexible because it can grow in size and overflow checks can be eliminated. If you had a *Basic Ada* or *Modula-2 mind-set*, you might implement a module or a package to encapsulate the data and hide the implementation details. If you had a more *Experienced Ada mind-set*, you might realize that a generic package could implement some form of polymorphism and that the package could be instantiated to work on any data type.

Finally, if you had an *Advanced Ada mind-set*, or more experience in the problem domain, then you might implement a family of generic packages. You could reuse the same interface and have several implementations tailored for certain domain-specific attributes. For instance, one version might allow concurrent operation—providing interlocks for resource contention. A second implementation might perform its own memory management—invoking a garbage collection process when required. These implementation choices are examples of how the language affects the abstraction.

SOFTWARE REUSE: THE SEARCH FOR ELEGANCE

Webster's dictionary [Mis87] defines **elegance** as:

> *"Tasteful richness of design—dignified gracefulness or restrained beauty in style, . . . scientific precision, or neatness, and simplicity."*

This definition could not be more appropriate for describing reusable software. Perhaps what has struck me most as I have poured over examples of reused software and analyzed why certain approaches are better than others is the fact that the most reusable software is often expressed the most elegantly. This software represents a *simple, clean abstraction* written in a representation that communicates its essence in a clear, concise manner.

Let me emphasize the *representation* aspect of reuse. This brings to mind the words of David Gries (at Cornell University), from his book *The Science of*

Programming [Gri89]. He writes that one should "Program into a programming language, not in it." Again, *language often limits what we can say and how elegantly we can say it.*

WHAT SETS REUSABLE SOFTWARE APART IS HOW IT IS PUT TOGETHER

This maxim captures two key aspects of software reuse:

1. the building block approach and

2. how things are glued together.

A key observation needs to be stated about developing systems from reusable components or building blocks. If one observes the software development process, one generally finds what is called *top-down functional decomposition*. But program construction with software components is typically a *bottom-up* process. There is a potential for conflict that surfaces in the next maxim.

TOP-DOWN VERSUS BOTTOM-UP REUSE

> *When you design your software* top-down, *but implement your software* bottom-up, *sometimes it doesn't meet in the middle.*

I've seen it happen! Furthermore, it doesn't just happen for designs. The same problem happens when systems analysts hand their requirements specifications over to software developers.

This communication problem leads nicely to the next series of observations.

WHEN YOUR OBJECT IS REUSABLE SOFTWARE YOU NEED A METHODOLOGY TO SUPPORT IT

This is a faintly veiled plug for *object-oriented software development*. Let me tell you why, in my opinion, an object-oriented design is the same as a good functional decomposition. Stevens, Meyers, and Constantine [SMC74], who first wrote about top-down functional decomposition, talked about *loosely coupled* modules that exhibit *strong cohesion*. By *loosely coupled* they meant, among other things, that the modules didn't directly reference any global data. By *strong cohesion* they meant that all the operations within a module were related, that they operated on the same logical data. These two characteristics are also attributes of objects developed using an object-oriented approach. An object encapsulates data and provides the *only operations for manipulating it*. Other attributes of object-oriented programming languages will be discussed in the sections that follow.

FOR INSTANCE, REUSABLE-SOFTWARE ENGINEERS INHERENTLY DO IT WITH CLASS

While I am focusing on object-oriented programming, I should mention three functional capabilities often available in object-oriented programming languages:

1. inheritance,

2. classes, and

3. instantiation.

Inheritance is transitive importation of function. If you declare module A to be visible to module B, then by default, the data and operations in module A are visible to any module that imports B.

Classes is another term for modules or packages. Classes are collections of operations (called "methods") on the data encapsulated within that class or within the class hierarchy. Note that classes may be parameterized.

Finally, *instantiation* is like macro expansion, except that your macro is a whole procedure or module. Instantiation is the mechanism whereby parameterized objects of a certain class are declared.

REUSABLE SOFTWARE: IT'S THE TYPE OF THING THAT MAKES IT MOST USEFUL

I contrived this maxim, to arrive at a play on the word *type*. A *type* is the type of thing that most of us typically take for granted. If one examines the evolution of types, you start with the following:

1. *Mathematics:* A type is an algebra. It defines a set of values and functions that map values of that type.

2. *Machine intrinsic types:* We have bits, addresses, and fixed point and floating point numbers and characters. These are the types the bare machine works on.

3. *Structured types:* Built into a language, such as Pascal, we have types such as an ARRAY, RECORD, FILE, SET, and STRING.

4. *User-defined (abstract) data types:* A language like Pascal also lets a programmer define enumerated types (e.g., red, orange, green), ranges, and give names to type REAL, INTEGER, BOOLEAN, and CHAR.

5. *Parameterized types:* A language like Ada [Ada83] allows you to specify types as parameters to generic units [Tra89].

6. *Polymorphic types:* Smalltalk [GR83] offers parameterized types where operations can be dynamically associated with a different type.

Using inheritance, you can create a type hierarchy of increasingly more generic functionality. Finally, in a language such as Ada, you can use derived types/subtypes to show the relationship between types and to emulate a weak form of inheritance.

SOFTWARE REUSE IS THE BEST WAY TO REUSE SOFTWARE AGAIN

Does this sound like a recursive definition? That is the point I am trying to make. When I went to college the first time, recursion was a theoretically attractive technique that lent itself to specifying *elegant algorithms* on paper, but that was it. Any machine implementation was slow. This is not true today. Compiler optimization of tail recursion can eliminate some of the context switching and activation record allocation overhead. Plus, having a function call itself is one form of internal reuse.

REUSABLE SOFTWARE HAS MANY ARGUMENTS; NONREUSABLE SOFTWARE MAY HAVE TOO MANY OR TOO FEW

As pointed out in Chapter 9, there is an appealing analogy between the time/space trade-offs associated with Reduced Instruction Set Computers versus Complex Instruction Set Computers as compared to Reduced Interface Software Components versus Complex Interface Software Components.

This analogy calls attention to what I consider to be one of the most crucial aspects in the development of reusable software: *interface design* [Mey82]. For example:

1. Which is a better subprogram abstraction—a procedure or a function?

2. What should the order of parameters be in a subprogram signature?

3. How can you design an interface that is most easily modified?

4. Should parameters have default values?

5. How should you handle errors?

6. Should you include just primitive operations in a module?

The subsections that follow provide some rationale for choosing answers to these questions.

No Functions Convention

If the use of a function subprogram construct is prohibited, then there will be no implicit "return" operand. Instead, all input and output parameters will appear in the parameter list.

Limit the Number of Parameters Convention

By limiting the number of parameters to each module, parameterization complexity is restricted. Similarly the potential adaptability is constrained. This limitation can be overcome through data encapsulation and the creation of two subprogram categories:

1. *Operations:* subprograms that perform operations on operands.

2. *Setup:* subprograms that set options (provide the context).

The advantage of this approach is that it facilitates the adaptability of the software. When a new option is determined, only a single subprogram needs to be added to control it, rather than modifying each existing subprogram to add a new parameter to its parameter list. Another advantage is that it keeps the number of parameters passed in each invocation to a minimum. (Note that defaults could exist to circumvent the number of parameters specified for each invocation, but this would not reduce the actual number of parameters passed.)

The disadvantage of this approach is the increased number of subprogram calls (and increased context switching effort at run time).

Parameter Ordering Convention

As described in the previous section, the two dominant forms of parameters are *operands* and *options*. The following conventions have been identified to guide the specification of a parameter list:

1. Operands should appear before options.

2. Operands that are modified should appear before operands that are referenced. This philosophy, in spirit, follows the traditional right-to-left assignment statement format.

3. Defaults should be provided for options whenever possible.

4. Options should be organized as an aggregate (record), thus simplifying the interface.

5. The setting of default values should be done under parametric control.

Internal Versus External Parameters

Parameters to modules may be passed at invocation through the conventional parameter list. Other mechanisms exist to gather parameter values at run time. These include

1. command line options (e.g., Unix options),

2. interactive solicitation for inputs in the form of values,

3. interactive solicitation for inputs in the form of option or operand *files*, and

4. explicit or implicit (standard input) default files for options or operands.

IT'S NOT EASY TO MAKE A GOOD CASE FOR SOFTWARE REUSE

Let me overstate my case—just in case you think reuse is not an open and shut case. I have a test case in my briefcase ready to showcase. It is about converting lowercase to uppercase, and it makes a good case in point. In any case, before I dismiss this case, I would like to make one more case for reuse.[3]

Seriously, I am talking about a computer-aided software engineering (CASE) environment for reuse. The best ones that I have seen are at MCC, where researchers have integrated a hypertext system [PB88] with a mail program to form a concurrent engineering distributed decision support tool, and at Xerox PARC (from the people who brought you the Smalltalk environment [GR83]), where they have integrated several forms of media on a workstation to facilitate

1. traceability (between requirements, design, and implementation into an information web [Asc91]),

2. knowledge capture (of design decisions, e.g., the graphical Issue Based Information System [KR79]),

3. multimedia representation (e.g., video and sound on a workstation), and

4. multiple windows with pull-down menus (e.g., the desktop paradigm).

REUSE—A UNIX EXPERIENCE

Picture this pipe dream:
Today's Menu: reuse—made to order.
Today's Special: macroni shell script delight.

I have really gone out of my way to tie in

1. Unix pipes,

2. shell scripts/execs,

3. macros, and

4. menus/panels.

These are some of the underlying technologies and techniques that facilitate reuse. I would especially like to emphasize the *reuse of processes*. Normally, when you talk about software reuse, you are thinking about reusing source code. Another form of reuse occurs when you write a shell script, a CMS (Conversational Monitoring System) exec, or a procedure for your JCL (Job Control

---

[3] The paragraph proves that puns are cheaper by the dozen.

Language); in these instances you are encapsulating and parameterizing a process for reuse. The same applies to menus and panels. They are shortcuts that minimize the number of keystrokes necessary to carry out a process.

HAVE TEMPLATE, WILL TRACE!

Actually, I cannot lay claim to the origination of this personal maxim. It was inflicted on me by the chair of the Penn State Computer Science Department, Preston Hammer, back in 1974 when flowchart templates were still in style. He thought that my name had a very computer-oriented ring.

I have included this maxim to call attention to a second form of reuse: reusable software templates (in artificial intelligence circles they may be called frames).

Code templates require a different mind-set from the building block, component development mind-set. It is sort of a *plan-for-change mind-set*. A template captures the basic control structure or architecture of a software component and leaves holes that need to be filled in before the unit can be used. The holes might have default values or can be parameterized. A template might be viewed as the glue into which building blocks can be put.

Paul Bassett's work at Netron, Inc., on frame technology [Bas87] demonstrates the commercial success of this approach. At Norma Industries, Ltd., frame technology has been demonstrated to result in a 90% reuse rate for the generation of large COBOL programs. These results are based on a relatively small number of procedural frames (less than 100) and a larger number of data-view frames (around 400).

JAPANESE SOFTWARE FACTORY MOTTO

Ask not what you can do for your software, but what your software can do for you.

This is what I call the Japanese software factory motto. It is the reason that they can justify the additional start-up costs for developing reusable software and creating the configuration management and library tools for the support environment. A Japanese software factory is just one example of the benefits of good domain analysis. They pick a business area where they know they can sell many customized systems; then they tool up to be competitive.

103

There is a corollary to this maxim:

What is one question that is never answered "no" more than once in a Japanese software factory?
Does a part exist that does this function?

However, the Japanese are interested not only in productivity improvements. They are, of course, pursuing reuse for another goal that can be summarized in the following section.

THE MOST IMPORTANT QUALITY OF REUSABLE SOFTWARE IS THAT IT IS QUALITY SOFTWARE

This maxim is derived from a remark made by Mitch Lubars while at MCC. It underscores the two *excuses* programmers most often cite for not reusing software:

1. How do I know if it works?

2. How do I know if I can make it work?

Whether the problem is an error of *commission* or *omission* made by the software developers in design or documentation, *quality* is the key to successful software reuse.

Let's look at an example (from *The Science of Programming* [Gri89]) of how bad things could be. Given a program made up of n components, what is the probability (P) that the program is correct? If one assumes that the probability that each component is correct is 95%, then if $n = 10$, the probability P that the entire program is correct is 60%. If $n = 100$, then the probability P is only 0.6%.

SOFTWARE REUSE, LIKE QUALITY, IS FREE

About five years ago Phillip Crosby published *Quality Is Free* [Cro79]. I would like to reuse the same analogy found in his book. You can pay for it now, or pay for it *again* later. In addition, *quality is free* when you reuse software because there is an increased chance that errors will be discovered the more the software is reused.

One final note. There has been discussion in the government pertaining to certain high flying programs (i.e., Star Wars) that might be difficult to maintain. One of the proposed *quality requirements* is that the system be composed of software that has been used at least *three* times.

YOU CAN MAKE THE DIFFERENCE BETWEEN REUSABLE SOFTWARE AND REUSED SOFTWARE

I believe that software reuse starts at home. It's the type of thing that you have been doing for a long time, and will continue to do. But, that doesn't mean that you can't share some of your expertise with others, or harness new technology. The problem is being *motivated* to do so.

There are two possible ways to encourage software reuse: First, *appeal to your ego:* "This is your chance to make a lasting contribution to the programming profession." Second, and probably more desirable, *appeal to your wallet or pocketbook:* For instance, there is the "Thief of the Week" award at Bell Labs where they reward individuals who exhibit the highest degree of reuse. (This brings to mind the story that transpired at a Bell Labs symposium on software reuse. When the "Thief of the Week" award concept was mentioned, someone in the audience remarked that there should be a "Victim of the Week" award also to acknowledge the efforts of the individual who created the software worthy of reuse in the first place.)

REUSABLE SOFTWARE ENGINEERING TECHNOLOGY

It's time to move from reusable software "techniques and mythology" to "technology and methodology."

In this chapter I have alluded to several techniques and technologies that facilitate software reuse. In closing I would like to summarize them for you. They will be treated in more detail in Chapter 19.

I have classified reusable software engineering technology into the following four areas:

1. methods,

2. tools,

3. languages, and

4. guidelines.

I realize that there may be some overlap in the categories, but I would like to leave this as a secondary issue. The *primary issue* is that these are the *current and future technologies* that have something to offer for software reuse.

The following software development methods or techniques lend themselves to reuse:

1. subroutines,

2. macros,

3. templates/frames,

4. application generators,

5. pipes/filters,

6. shell scripts/execs,

7. abstraction (data, procedural, and control),

8. layers of abstraction,

9. information hiding,

10. AI expert systems, analogical reasoning,

11. spiral software development model/rapid prototyping,

12. object-oriented design, and

13. programming by difference.

The following list of tools support software reuse:

1. CASE,

2. menus/panels,

3. library/repository mechanisms,

4. hypertext,

5. theorem provers/quality of formal methods, and

6. object-oriented and wide-spectrum programming languages.

The following is a list of programming language features that influence the development of reusable software:

1. types,

2. coercion,

3. overloading,

4. parameterized types/generics,

5. classes/packages/modules,

6. inheritance/importation,

7. parameter passing mechanisms, and

8. recursion.

Finally, guidelines and standards are essential for increasing the generation of reusable software. They address the following aspects of software development:

1. domain analysis,

2. design,

3. code,

4. documentation,

5. legal issues (protecting assets),

6. management, and

7. test.

REUSABLE SOFTWARE IS A GOOD EXAMPLE OF SOFTWARE ENGINEERING DISCIPLINE

Software reuse is not an end in itself, but a means to an end. I believe that the only way the full potential of software reuse can be achieved is through a disciplined approach to software development that incorporates as many as possible of the technologies I have cited in the previous section. Until then, we will be facing ad hoc (or a better term might be odd hack) reuse, or just business as re-usual.

MYTHS REVISITED...

Chapter 17

Software Reuse Myths

THIS CHAPTER[1] analyzes nine commonly believed software reuse myths. These myths reveal certain technical, organizational, and psychological software engineering research issues and trends. These myths partially explain why software reuse has not had, to date, the broad sweeping effects envisioned by the programming prophets. The myths are as follows:

1. Software reuse is a technical problem.

2. Special tools are needed for software reuse.

3. Reusing code results in huge increases in productivity.

4. Artificial intelligence will solve the reuse problem.

5. The Japanese have solved the reuse problem.

6. Ada has solved the reuse problem.

7. Designing software from reusable parts is like designing hardware using integrated circuits.

8. Reused software is the same as reusable software.

9. Software reuse will just happen.

Each of these myths is examined individually in the sections that follow. The analysis is in two parts:

1. the "original" analysis as it appeared in 1987 and

---

[1] Portions of this material are found in *ACM Software Engineering Notes* (January 1988), in *Software Reuse: Emerging Technology* (April 1987, IEEE Computer Society Press), and *Proceedings of the 16th International Conference on Software Engineering* (May 1994).

2. the "revisited" analysis in light of technology advances made up to and including 1994.

MYTH #1: SOFTWARE REUSE IS A TECHNICAL PROBLEM

Original Analysis

Many good people have been led astray by assuming that the software reuse problem needs a technical solution. Although there are both technical and nontechnical barriers inhibiting software reuse, if one looks at the most-often-stated reasons why software is not reused [Tra86], the overwhelming majority of them may be classified as psychological, sociological, or economic. The only technical reasons cited are the lack of search methods to find the right pieces or the lack of quality components (to put in the library in the first place) to reuse.

In the latter case, management plays a critical role in setting and enforcing standards, as well as motivating programmers to develop components and to design software based on them. The library issue will be addressed in the following myth. Finally, as stated by Ratcliffe [Rat87], ". . . the whole western economic system may be against reuse." The development of software reuse has been stunted by intracompany and intercompany legal, contractual, and political conflicts.

Revisited Analysis

Three major nontechnical impediments to reuse have diminished somewhat during the last six years. Some consensus-building efforts have focused on coming up with standard definitions for reuse and reusability. The Reuse Interoperability Group (RIG), for example, is attempting to come up with standards for reusable components and their interchange through common library access methods [TC93a]. Furthermore, recent efforts within the DoD to change government acquisition policies will further stimulate the industry [Pip92]. Finally, with copyright law now being reinterpreted by the courts [Sam90] to allow for more flexibility in developing plug-compatible solutions (that may have some common design structure but no common code), the software marketplace is poised to better be served by competitive, commercial, off-the-shelf (COTS) offerings for reuse.

On the technical side, research in process programming, persistent object bases, and knowledge representation and manipulation show the potential for facilitating the creation of fertile reuse environments. (See Chapter 19 for a more detailed description of the impact of these technologies on software reuse.) The success of ARPA's Domain-Specific Software Architecture (DSSA) program [Met90, GM92] also provides valuable credibility to reuse in general.

MYTH #2: SPECIAL TOOLS ARE NEEDED FOR SOFTWARE REUSE

Original Analysis

The term *special* is meant to imply tools tailored specifically to facilitate the reusable software engineering process. When reviewing the tools proposed to support software reuse, researchers generally include a library facility and perhaps a standards-checking program or syntax-directed editor. If one examines some of the most cited successful applications of software reuse (e.g., [LG84] and [MSN⁺81]), one finds that few, if any, tools at all are used. The Japanese software factories use a simple Key Word In Context (KWIC) index to locate the desired function. Furthermore, production software libraries seldom exceed 100 to 200 components in size, a number that is very easily managed manually by most programmers. (There are instances of very large repositories of subroutines as with the National Bureau of Standards Library, which contains more than 2800 entries. In this case, a library system is a necessity.) In the instances where prototype reusable software libraries have been developed, they have either been created using a relational database system [BB85, Onu87], or an information retrieval system [FG90]. Finally, in most instances of software reuse, programmers modify existing programs, written by themselves or by a programmer on the same project [GN86]. In this case, because of the proximity and accessibility to the resource, the programmer does not need a sophisticated tool to locate the software to reuse.

Revisited Analysis

Integrated CASE tools, when they get here, have the potential to enhance software reuse. While they are not necessary for reuse, they do go a long ways toward making reuse fun. They will facilitate the traceability of requirements to design and code, along with the other artifacts associated with software development. Reusable software can be thought of as a CASE tool in itself in that reusable software components are just another tool that should be leveraged in solving problems (as mentioned in Chapter 3). DSSAs [GM92] are a step in the right direction, assuming that they are integrated with a CASE environment. Furthermore, with the reduction in cost of multimedia in workstations, new, user-friendly environments will be appearing by the turn of the century that should revolutionize the way software is developed and take "end-user computing" closer to reality.

MYTH #3: REUSING CODE RESULTS IN HUGE INCREASES IN PRODUCTIVITY

Original Analysis

What is *huge*? Studies have shown [HM84] that even if 40% of a design and 75% of the code on a given project is reused, the resulting 50% reduction in testing, and comparable reductions in integration test, documentation, and system test, result in a net productivity gain of only 40%. To achieve an order-of-magnitude improvement in software productivity, one must resort to application generators, or highly parameterized components. (Still, cutting software development time roughly in half is not bad.) The real payoff is realized by the decreased maintenance costs! Maintenance cost reductions of up to 90% have been reported when reusable code, code templates, and application generators have been used to develop new systems.

On the other hand, one cannot ignore the initial start-up costs. Software designed for reuse costs between 20% and 25% more to develop and learn to use.[2] The break-even point is not reached until after the second or third use.

Revisited Analysis

There has been a lack of good empirical data related to reuse success stories. There really should be more data out in the literature, but there isn't. While it is true that, in some instances, reuse has been shown to result in a 20 to 1 reduction in effort for "certain" stages in the development life cycle [BS92],

---

[2] I have chosen to leave in this optimistic projection on my part, made in 1987. Little did I realize how domain specific the answer to this question was. Empirical data gathered to date (I should say "offered to date") shows that software that is designed, documented, and supported for reuse costs up to 200% more than one-shot solutions.

this should be placed in perspective with the "cost" of reuse. Three costs are associated with reuse:

1. the cost of making something reusable,

2. the cost of reusing it, and

3. the cost of defining and implementing a reuse process.

Focusing on the *cost of making software reusable*, a conservative breakdown is as follows:

25%	for additional generalization,
15%	for additional documentation,
15%	for additional testing, and
5%	for library support and maintenance.
60%	additional cost of making something reusable.

The subtle and sad thing about it is that reusability is quite subjective. Who can say that spending x% on documentation will make it y% more reusable, or an additional z% spent generalizing will make it q% more reusable? Obviously, you don't just "spend the money"; you focus it on making certain attributes of the software "better."

Finally, there is the *cost to reuse software*. The empirical data I have seen pretty much all center around a 5 to 1 ratio (five lines of reused code costs the same as one line of newly developed code) [Tra87c]. This is all homogenized though, because the first time you reuse something, it's going to cost you more to find it, understand how to use it, etc. Obviously, if you have to modify it, it will cost you more still. Selby has reported a 20 to 1 or 25 to 1 ratio for black box reuse versus white box that drops dramatically when 5% or less of the code has been modified [Sel91].

MYTH #4: ARTIFICIAL INTELLIGENCE WILL SOLVE THE REUSE PROBLEM

Original Analysis

How can we automate something we have no expertise in? Actually such a statement is not entirely fair, because AI does have something to offer. There are strong similarities between the problem domain analysis performed by systems analysts trying to extract common components for reuse in similar applications and the domain analysis performed by heuristic search algorithms trying to match requirement specifications to program frames or schemas. However, automatic generation of code from requirements is still a research area. Expert systems have been designed to assist programmers in locating components [Bra86] that match desired functions, and instantiate them [McN86], but the lack of a good notation to represent the semantics of software is still the major roadblock to unleashing the power of AI approaches.

Revisited Analysis

I have always been skeptical of "imitation intelligence." Recently, through my involvement in the ARPA DSSA community, I have become convinced that software reuse is the common ground where AI and software engineering will meet. It is becoming more and more apparent that one needs to reuse more than just code to gain increased benefits from reuse. AI, with its knowledge acquisition and representation experience, has a lot to offer to support this kind of reuse. In fact, machine learning and knowledge acquisition closely resemble application generators and domain analysis—both fundamental to software reuse.

MYTH #5: THE JAPANESE HAVE SOLVED THE REUSE PROBLEM

Original Analysis

Many hold the somewhat mystical belief that the Japanese have solved the (fill in the blank) problem. The success of the Japanese software factories is not based on any technological breakthroughs, but on the formalization of the process and the product. A question that gets answered "no" only once in a Japanese software factory is "Does a part exist that performs this function?" (As originally discussed in Chapter 16.) Japanese programmer training and sense of commitment to standards also strongly facilitate reusable software engineering.

Another reason for the success of the Japanese software factory may be summarized in the following paraphrased motto: "Ask not what you can do for your software, but what your software can do for you." By making a business decision to address a particular problem domain and recognizing the leverage software reuse plays, the Japanese have justified amortizing the cost of developing the *critical mass* of reusable software and the associated software engineering environment ultimately necessary to succeed.

Revisited Analysis

The Japanese continue to do good things by taking an evolutionary rather than revolutionary approach. They have recognized the nontechnical inhibitors to software reuse and have invested in creating the assets and processes to support reuse. As I have previously stated, "Before you can reuse software, you need software to reuse." They have addressed this issue head on, though they haven't declared victory yet.

MYTH #6: ADA HAS SOLVED THE REUSE PROLBLEM

Original Analysis

Writing a generic package in Ada does not necessarily make it reusable any more than writing a FORTRAN subroutine or assembly language macro. The adaptability (and reuse potential) of a software component depends on the amount of domain analysis performed and the degree a module is parameterized to reflect this. Furthermore, the type of parameterization facilities provided by the programming language may not always support the degree or form of adaptability desired, as is the case with Ada generics. The same holds for a class in Smalltalk or other object-oriented languages. While certain language features do facilitate the development of reusable software, the language, in itself, is not enough to solve the problem.

Revisited Analysis

Ada has not, and will not go away. Ada continues to be the language of "no choice" for DoD contractors. Ada 9X [Ada89] has made claims to have increased support for reusability in the form of an anemic inheritance mechanism and object types (but it still lends itself to improvement as well as abuse).

As far as a language that promotes reuse goes, C++ [Str86], baroque[3] as it is, has almost become the de facto standard. Because of the sheer volume of

---

[3] In fact, in the words of Doug Lea, with all its quirky language features, C++ has become "baroque-n." C++ compilers don't support some of the best reuse constructs (e.g., virtual bases, templates, exceptions) very well (or at all), so people don't use them.

software being written in the language, there are more reusable C++ components available than in any other language. That doesn't mean that it is the best language in which to write reusable software.[4] It does contain a minimal set of object-oriented language constructs (i.e., inheritance, delegation, frameworks, and contracts), but still does not provide for good separation of interface inheritance from code inheritance/delegation.

MYTH #7: DESIGNING SOFTWARE FROM REUSABLE PARTS IS LIKE DESIGNING HARDWARE USING INTEGRATED CIRCUITS

Original Analysis

Why don't software building blocks exist that programmers can wire together to build systems, similar to the way it is done for integrated circuits? If they did exist, what type of CASE environment would be necessary to support them? Are electrical engineers that much smarter than software engineers? Superficially, comparing software design and hardware design [Cox86] is a very appealing analogy. At one level of complexity, the analogy holds. Structured programming relies on a select handful of basic structures. (For example, an "if statement" is similar to a two-way multiplexor. A "for loop" is like a counter.) Unfortunately, the analogy breaks down [Pol86] when one realizes that both the number and the complexity of software components far exceeds those currently used by logic designers. Because of the variety of applications, the wide spectrum of problem-domain-specific components, and, most of all, the amount of "glue" necessary to connect software components, the similarities between software and hardware design have yet to be fully exploited. Other hard problems include identifying the building blocks, defining (and documenting) the interfaces, and parameterizing the components. Finally, economic factors differentiate hardware design from software design. For practical reasons, hardware designers must constrain their design to be based on available components, whereas software designers can create designs based on custom components. Furthermore, unused functionality in a hardware chip doesn't affect the chip's performance, whereas excess code can affect program size as well as performance.

---

[4] Andy Koenig at Bell Labs likes to point out that the difference between Ada and C++ is that "programmers don't have to program in C++."

Revisited Analysis

I have waivered on the position I took on this point five years ago, because the analogy of component-based software design and component-based hardware design is conveniently seductive. (Yes, Brad Cox, I hate to admit you may be right with your software–IC analogy [Cox87, Cox90a, Cox90b].) The big "if" that makes me want to agree with the analogy is "if software interfaces were defined as crisply as hardware interfaces" then I would believe the myth is true, especially in light of all the object-oriented religious fervor that has been so popular of late. But, of course, there are no catalogs of components, outside of user interface widgits. The reason may still lie in the immaturity of the science, or in that we do not understand the complexity of integration. Said another way, we don't understand the types of glue/solder that are needed to connect the components together, nor do we have standard bus protocols to let us hook up larger components.

MYTH #8: REUSED SOFTWARE IS THE SAME AS REUSABLE SOFTWARE

Original Analysis

A corollary to this myth is "A good way to develop reusable software is to take an existing program and add parameters." Both these myths fail to emphasize the need to design for and document for reuse. Unplanned reuse of software (also called software salvaging) occurs frequently in the software community. Programmers often extract modules or code segments and then modify them to meet their needs. This is an error-prone and time-consuming process, which could be avoided if the software were initially designed with reuse in mind. As the corollary implies, reuse should be considered at design time, not after the implementation has been completed. The emphasis should be on *planned* reuse. Special attention needs to be placed on interface design and modularization (e.g., low coupling and high cohesion [SMC74]).

Revisited Analysis

This point needs no discussion. With several reuse standards for "designing software for reuse" available [BGE85, Den86, Wea86], it is testimony that reusability, like quality, is an attribute of software that must be planned. It is refreshing to see that the government is finally recognizing the difference between "unplanned/opportunistic" reuse, which it (and others in industry) calls "salvaging," and "planned" reuse [GAO93].

Finally, in reality, not all reusable software is initially "planned." Some reusable software components are the result of reengineering efforts [AF93], where, through repackaging and redocumenting, software can be cost-effectively reengineered into reusable components.

MYTH #9: SOFTWARE REUSE WILL JUST HAPPEN

Original Analysis

Judging from the limited success software reuse has enjoyed to date, most software reuse is not planned; therefore, the full potential has not been realized. Yet, times are changing. As hardware costs decrease and performance increases, customers are becoming less willing to buy a costly customized piece of software when a slightly more inefficient (due to some overhead in parameterization) but less costly software may do. To reach this goal, components need to be designed, documented, and implemented for reuse [BHR+92] according to some guidelines [Wea86, DSFO86]. Finally, management needs to provide the incentives to motivate and reward the application of this technology [Tra87c].

Revisited Analysis

In six years' time, reuse has been given a lot of press, but it really has not blossomed. I am encouraged by the DoD initiatives, for example, ARPA STARS (Software Technology for Adaptable, Reliable Systems) [STA92], ARPA's DSSA [GM92], and the DISA CIM (Defense Information Systems Agency Corporate Information Management) effort [Pip92]. I am also pleased by the progress HP [Gri91, Gri93a] and IBM [TG93] have made at institutionalizing software reuse as part of the corporate programming strategy.

Finally, recent interest in Visual Basic VBX and OCX sockets [Ude94] and the availability of class libraries have shown the increased sophistication of the commercial marketplace for integration standards. VBX-like standards, OLE (object linking and embedding), and CORBA (common object request broker) have the potential to foster a component industry.

The bottom line is that software reuse is maturing. It has learned to crawl and in the next five years, may even walk upright without dragging its knuckles.

CONCLUSION

The material in this chapter represents one perspective on why software reuse has not played a major role in improving programmer productivity. The realities of the myths discussed are as follows:

1. Software reuse is a technical and nontechnical problem.

2. No "special" tools are needed for software reuse. Available database technology can be applied to help organize and retrieve software in large repositories.

3. Reusing code alone will not result in an order-of-magnitude increase in productivity and quality.

4. Artificial intelligence technology can play a role in solving the reuse problem.

5. The Japanese have taken the first steps toward solving the reuse problem.

6. No single language alone can solve the reuse problem.

7. Designing software from reusable parts is not like designing hardware using integrated circuits.

8. Reusing software that was not planned for reuse is harder than reusing software that was designed for reuse.

9. Software reuse will not just happen.

While reusable software cannot solve the software crisis by itself, it has the potential to make a significant impact [Bro87]. By exposing the preconceived myths about software reuse, the material in this chapter should help programmers and managers direct their efforts and resources more effectively and, thus, achieve more readily the goal of reusable software engineering.

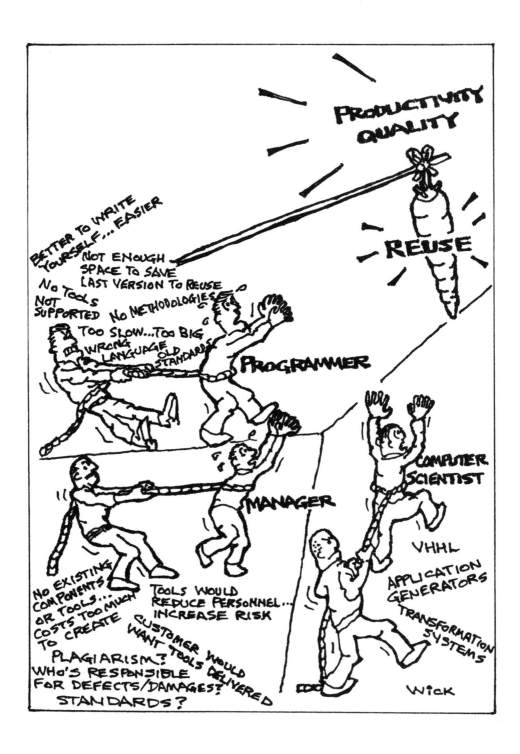

Chapter 18

Software Reuse Motivators and Inhibitors

THE SOFTWARE engineering community is showing a renewed interest in software reuse. The search for quality and productivity has brought about attempts to apply manufacturing technology to programming. This chapter[1] summarizes the inhibitors of software reuse and analyzes the limited success that it has enjoyed. Technical, organizational, political, psychological, and economic issues related to software reuse are addressed.

INTRODUCTION

This chapter examines three issues:

1. Why the paradigm of reusable software engineering is desirable.

2. Why it has not had, to date, the broad sweeping effects envisioned by the programming prophets.

3. Why it has enjoyed, under certain circumstances, limited success.

The goal of this chapter is to identify, summarize, and analyze the technical, organizational, political, psychological, and economic motivators and inhibitors associated with software reuse. By consolidating these factors, a clearer picture of the dependencies and interactions is created. This chapter is organized into three sections. The first section elaborates on the two main motivations for reusing software: *productivity* and *quality*. The second section addresses the question "What makes reusing software artifacts (e.g., code,

---

[1] Portions of this material were derived from *Software Reuse: Motivators and Inhibitors* [Tra87c]. For other good references on this topic see [GFP93] or [Fra93].

designs, documentation, or test cases) difficult?" This question is answered from the perspective of a

1. programmer,

2. software manager,

3. computer scientist, and

4. cognitive psychologist.

The last section summarizes some often-cited industrial experience in software reuse. The limited success of software reuse for programming-in-the-small is contrasted with the much more publicized Japanese software factories' accomplishments.

WHY REUSABLE SOFTWARE SHOULD BE

Before one addresses the technical and economic reasons of why software should be reused, it is important to gain a perspective on recent advances in the state of the practice. Current software engineering technology has focused on improving workstation performance, generating friendly user interfaces, and integrating environments. Assuming that these goals will be attained in the near future, the key issue becomes "What is next? How can we find a way to make programmers an order of magnitude more productive?" Barring any immediate breakthroughs in artificial intelligence, the next frontier appears to be software reuse. Although CASE tools may improve productivity by allowing you to do portions of the development process faster, software reuse completely eliminates portions of the development effort.

Advantages of Software Reuse

The two major reasons for reusing software are *productivity* and *quality*. Systems developed based on reusable software artifacts, in principle, should cost less (which is partially attributable to a shorter schedule) and contain fewer defects because of the "tried and true" parts of which it is composed. Productivity and quality will be individually addressed in the sections that follow.

Productivity.   Gains in productivity reduce development costs and schedule time. Software reuse increases productivity for these reasons:

- Software reuse "amplifies" programming capabilities [BP84]. The programmer has fewer symbols to write when large portions of the code or design are copied verbatim.

- Software reuse reduces the amount of documentation and testing required.

- A synergistic effect occurs when systems are developed based on reusable components. The system becomes easier to maintain and modify because the software developers are more familiar with the reusable building blocks from which it is constructed and can more rapidly understand the complete system design.

Finally, software development based on reusable building blocks offers opportunities for increased system performance when frequently used components are migrated into microcode, special hardware, or silicon.

Quality. Improvements in quality from developing software based on reusable components can be attributed to the following characteristics of reused software:

- It is well designed (i.e., designed for reuse).

- It is well documented—conforming to an established standard.

- It is well tested—certified for reuse. The more software is reused, the greater the probability an error will not be found. (That is, if any errors existed in the code, they would have been found by previous users.)

- Its function is well understood and likely to be used appropriately.

One of the quality benefits that is achieved when developing software based on reusable software artifacts comes through rapid prototyping. Rapid prototyping allows for system concepts and user interfaces to be demonstrated earlier in the development cycle, thus reducing costly rework during later phases.

WHY REUSABLE SOFTWARE ISN'T

"What makes reusing software artifacts difficult?" The answers to this question depend on many technical, organizational, political, and psychological issues. This section contains a discussion of the inhibitors identified with reusable software presented from four points of view:

1. *Programmer*: someone who designs, implements and tests a portion of a software system.

2. *Software manager*: someone who manages a software development project.

3. *Computer scientist*: someone on the leading edge of technology who is exploring and developing new techniques for expanding the reusable software engineering paradigm.

4. *Cognitive psychologist*: someone who understands the human thought process, its limitations, and implications for programming.

A Programmer's Viewpoint

What are some of the reasons why a programmer doesn't use someone else's code or design?

- It is more fun to write it oneself.

- It would imply a sign of weakness not to be able to do it oneself.

- It is not "*my* code." This is part of the NIH (Not Invented Here) syndrome of making oneself indispensable to assure job security.

- It is easier to write it oneself than to try to locate it, figure out what it does, and find out if it works. If it has to be modified, then it also might be easier to rewrite it from scratch.

- It is perceived by the programmer that it is cheaper to write software from scratch, rather than to tailor a design to leverage existing artifacts.

- There was not enough shelf space or disk space to save the last version to reuse.

- There are no tools to help find components or compose a system from the reusable pieces.

- There are no software development methods that stress reusing code, let alone reusing a design or a specification.

- There was no consideration by the system analyst, who specified the system, that portions of an existing system could be salvaged and reused.

- There is little emphasis on reusing software taught in academia [Den81]; in fact, most students don't have any mechanism or motivation to save programs from assignment to assignment, let alone, from course to course.

- The code or artifact in question is not supported (If a bug is found, no one will fix it, or assist in determining the cause.); executes too slowly; has parameters of the wrong data type; is too big;[2] is written in the wrong language; was written in the right language on a different processor (Is it transportable?); or was not developed according to current standards.

The issues raised in this section are both technical and psychological. The technical issues raised focus on the lack of well-described, useful, and reliable reusable component libraries and an integrated programming environment available to take advantage of them. On the psychological side, the reluctance of a programmer to retool and place a dependence on someone else's work generally inhibits initial acceptance of this approach.

A Manager's Viewpoint

Managers often make decisions based on more than just technical issues. Some reasons for not adopting a reusable software engineering approach for a software project might be as follows:

- If no tools or components exist, then it will take time and labor to create the tools and components and to gain the expertise in their use. Such costs are generally not within the budget of a single project [Jon86].

- If the tools do exist for making programmers more productive, then this will make the project more dependent on fewer personnel. Decreasing the number of experts in a project increases the impact (and risk factor) of losing an employee due to illness (the Mac truck theory). Finally, any

---

[2]The larger an artifact is, the more benefit will result from its reuse, but the less likely it is to fit into an application without changes [PD85].

reduction in headcount might be perceived as reducing the empire a manager commands [RH83].

- If special tools (e.g., application generators or preprocessors) are used to create a program, then a customer might expect these tools to be delivered along with the product for maintenance purposes.

- If systems are built that incorporate proprietary reusable components, how is the proprietary software protected from being plagiarized in delivered systems?

- If a defect appears in a program developed using reused components, who is legally responsible [Tra91b] for damages?

- If there are no standards to control what is entered into the components library [CP83], then time and money must be spent setting and maintaining the standards.

Finally, there are no economic or other types of incentives for creating reusable components [Jon86]. If a contractor delivers a reusable/adaptable piece of software, then the chances of follow-on or maintenance work are reduced. Furthermore, technical issues faced by management are sometimes tainted by political considerations or personal aspirations. Nevertheless, a certain amount of experience in budgeting, scheduling, and managing a software project based on a reusable components library is necessary before any confidence can be placed in the method.

A Computer Scientist's Viewpoint

Computer scientists have the luxury of taking a broader perspective when addressing the issue of reusability than programmers faced with existing schedules and budgets. "Used Program Sales and Service" isn't a likely dissertation topic. Balzer [Sta84] has stated that "Code is not reusable."[3] He suggested that instead of the black box, plug-compatible approach that is focused on programming *products*, the answer to reusable software lies in analyzing the programming *process*. From this perspective, Horowitz and Munson [HM84] have suggested the following alternative approaches to reusability:

---

[3] The rationale for this statement comes from a belief that there is no clear advantage for code reuse if you have to take the time to read it, test it, and perhaps modify it before you are sure it will provide the functionality that you need. Obviously, this statement is contradictory to common belief. Black box reuse is highly successful, not only in software but in hardware design.

- *Very high level languages* (VHLLs) allow specification of problem domain entities and operations directly in the syntax of the language. Similarly, problem-oriented languages (POLs) are a form of VHLL specifically tailored for a particular problem domain. Reusability is accomplished by reusing the compiler.

- *Application generators* are software tools that create programs given a parameterized or programmed specification. Reusability is accomplished by reusing the application generator for each new problem.

- *Transformation systems* require that high-level specifications be written describing *what* the software system should do. The specifications are then transformed by a series of pattern-matching expansions into a program [Che84].

The key concept in each of these three examples focuses on the automated application of reusable components. Each tool recognizes some type of high-level pattern in the problem domain that can be implemented by substituting some (parameterized) code fragments. Certain theoretical limits of the transformational techniques have been investigated.

A Cognitive Psychologist's Viewpoint

Computer programming is simply one form of problem solving. Understanding the merits of existing programming paradigms from the perspective of cognitive psychology [Tra79] has provided valuable insight in dealing with complexity. Reusable software has been the focus of studies by Soloway and Ehrlich [SE84] and Curtis [Cur83]. A summary of the empirical evidence gathered as it applies to reusable software engineering follows:

- The size of short-term memory limits the number (7 ± 2) [Mil56] of pieces of information one can manipulate consciously at one moment in time. This limit on complexity can be overcome by proper *chunking* or modularization of components, that is, by collecting units of information into one semantically meaningful piece (or package). (*Note*: This argument supports information hiding and object-oriented design [PCW83], two paradigms that are useful when creating reusable components.)

- Expert (i.e., experienced) programmers develop applications through a recursive mental process [JTPA81] of matching pieces of the problem with solution segments with which they are familiar (e.g., plans [SE83]). Therefore, subconsciously, portions of designs are reused each time a program is written.

- Internal conceptualization of the knowledge base in which program/ design segments reside tends to evolve with experience into having a uniform content for all programmers [MRRH81]. In other words, experienced programmers tend to think alike and express their solutions in similar forms.

- Programmers cannot reuse something they don't understand. Furthermore, expert programmers follow certain explicit *rules of discourse* [SE84] regarding naming conventions and programming style [KP78] that enhance program readability and comprehension. This implies that for something to be reused, it has to be well written, and documented according to an accepted standard.

These observations support the need for a proper programming environment to facilitate the reusable software engineering paradigm. Tools must be available to handle the complexity and assist the programmer in understanding what software components exist. These results also demonstrate the intuitive validity of such an approach.

WHY REUSABLE SOFTWARE IS

Software reuse has met with some limited success. However, advances in the state of the practice have been slow and sporadic. This section analyzes circumstances under which software has been reused. Two environments will be examined:

1. programming-in-the-small (i.e., small software projects) and

2. software factories.

Programming-in-the-Small

A majority of the software developed in the United States is written by individuals or small teams of programmers associated with a single project or product. Software is reused for the following reasons:

- It was written by the person who is reusing it.

- It was written by another person in the project.

- An application is being developed where a previous version or a similar program is available.

- The software is for a function that is well understood, only has a few data types, relies on a stable underlying technology (i.e., I/O), and has standards within the problem domain [BR87a]. Scientific subroutines are examples of this type of software.

- It was mandated by the manager to do so.

- It was determined by the developer to be to his advantage, either financially[4] or technically.

Finally, some programmers view developing reusable software as being a chance to become immortal, a chance to put the ego back in programming.

Software Factories

The Japanese have taken a different approach to programming; instead of software development, they view it as software production. They can cite up to an order of magnitude more programming productivity for the following reasons:

- They have established a critical mass in the number of reusable components (>1000) and programmers available to use and develop them.

- They have taken the separate phases in the software development process and assigned them to different organizations within the software factory.

- They have developed an integrated set of tools and rigid standards to support reuse in the software production life cycle. Because of the large numbers of programmers using the tools, their initial development cost can be economically justified.

- Their management is committed to this approach.

---

[4]In certain locations at IBM, programmers could receive up to several thousand dollars for "cost avoidance" through their facilities' software reuse incentive program.

- Software reuse is part of their training process. One software factory [TM84] gave programming exercises each month to all its programmers. These exercises required programmers to reference the library of reusable components so that they could complete them with the minimum of effort.

The average programmer productivity in the United States is 100 to 500 source lines of code (SLOC) per month [Jon84] of new and reused code. The average programmer productivity in a Japanese software factory is 500 to 800 SLOC/month [Mat84] of new code, and 800 to 3200 SLOC/month of new and reused code.

The following list contains additional productivity/quality figures derived from various Japanese software engineering efforts during the last 20 years. While they have not been normalized to allow for variances in programming languages, they do reflect an impressive trend.

- Toshiba (1976): 1390 SLOCS/month

- Toshiba (1979): 13% reuse rate

- Toshiba (1981): 2870 SLOCS/month; 65% reuse rate with 0.3 defects/ KSLOC

- Toshiba (1985): 3100 SLOCS/month; 48% reuse rate [Mat87]

- Toshiba (1985): greater than 30% reuse rate using TFF (technical description formula for 50SM design) [MT93]

- Toshiba (1986): 2000 SLOCS/month; 65% reuse rate with 0.3 defects/ KSLOC [CK90]

- Toshiba (1986): 4.5M EASL (equivalent assembly source lines) per month; 55% to 60% reuse ratio [Mat86]

- Toshiba (1990): 30% reuse ratio on applications with parts outside the domain that the parts were originally designed for [MYTT90]

- Toshiba (1990): 60% to 80% reuse ratio inside application domain [MYTT90]

- Toshiba (1991): 20% to 30% bug reduction; 60% reuse ratios [Mat91]

- Hitachi (1984): use of EAGLE (effective approach to achieving high-level software productivity); 22 standard patterns and 16 parts for batch processing with 9 patterns and 60 parts for on-line processing; resulted in reuse ratio of 68%, a 2× productivity improvement and error reduction of two-thirds [MT93].

- Hitachi (1986): increase in productivity of 2.3× with software parts

- Hitachi (1986): increase in productivity of 4.5× with program generator

- Hitachi (1988): increase in productivity of 2 to 3× with reusable logic frames

- Hitachi (1988): 80% reuse coverage in small office applications

- Hitachi (1989): FREICT reduced workload one-half to one-eighth; Parts creation tool reduced workload by 90%.

- Hitachi (1991): 81% generation using EAGLE2 (73% to 98%) [TMTT92]

- NEC (1986): increase in productivity of 1.1 to 1.2× with software parts

- NEC (1986): increase in productivity of 1.2 to 10× with standard logic parts

- NEC (1992): 70% coverage with SEA/I generator; yielded 10× improvement [MHK+91]

- NEC (1992): 90% reuse on typical application using SEA/I generator [MHK+91]

- NTT (1988): reuse ratio 16% and deposition ratio 9.8% [Iso92]

- NTT (1990): reuse ratio saturated 20% [Iso92]

- Fujitsu (1984): 10 common modules account for 80% of code in 100 modules [MT93]

- Fujitsu (1989): design workload reduction 30PM ⇒ 10PM ⇒ 2PM (interface design reuse)

- Fujitsu (1991): using YPS/APG, productivity improved by 1.3 to 1.5×.

CONCLUSION

This chapter has described the difficulties faced by programmers and program managers who attempt to reuse software artifacts and the motivation for overcoming them. The limited areas of success have also been discussed. The major issues can be summarized as follows:

- The primary factors motivating the reuse of software are productivity and quality.

- Most programmers tend to view reusability from the perspective of simply reusing code, whereas reusing other programming artifacts (e.g., designs, specifications, and tests) leads to more productivity. Furthermore, other reusability paradigms (e.g. application generators, translation systems, VHLLs, and POLs) have proven successful [HM84].

- Meaningful, properly documented, tested, verified, and classified reusable components need to be developed before they can be reused [DSFO86, Sta84].

- Expert (i.e., experienced) programmers with an understanding of the problem domain and the contents of a component library are best suited to fully exploit the reusable software engineering paradigm [SE84].

- Tools and methods are needed to support the development and cataloging of reusable components and the composing of software systems from them [CP83]. (The emphasis here is on the methods, more than on the tools. That is, design and documentation standards need to be established and supported by design for reuse and design for reuse processes.)

- A component-based approach introduces real or perceived staffing risks associated with the increased dependence on a single individual to do the work of many [RH83].

- Reusable software development systems cost money, time, and manpower to develop and become proficient at using.

- Software is most likely to be reused if it is geographically close to the originator.

- This feasibility of software reuse has been demonstrated by the Japanese software factories partly because of the concentration of programmers (critical mass), which maximizes their return on tool investment.

Wegner's [Weg83] adage "We should stand on each others shoulders, not on each others feet" aptly describes the potential of software reuse. The computer industry is faced with a software crisis, a predicted shortage of programmers, and the fact that software productivity has increased only 3% to 8% a year over the last 30 years [Boe81]. Studies on reuse have shown that:

- 40% to 60% of all code is reusable from one application to another [BP84],

- 60% of the design and code on all business applications is reusable [LG84],

- 75% of program functions are common to more than one program, and

- only 15% of the code found in most programs is unique and novel to a specific application [Jon84].

Software reuse will continue to be a topic of research and technology infusion for the rest of the century. The factors brought out here, once recognized and properly addressed, should assist in facilitating the institutionalization of software reuse.

Chapter 19

Software Reuse Technical Opportunities

ONE OF the dilemmas that has prevented software developers from reusing software is the lack of software artifacts to use or the existence of artifacts that are difficult to locate, understand, adapt, and integrate (they are more or less reuseless). This chapter's goal is to identify technical opportunities for software researchers that will lead to the availability of high-quality, easy to locate, easy to understand, easy to adapt, and easy to integrate "reusable" software components.[1]

INTRODUCTION

"If I have seen further it is by standing on the shoulders of giants."

—Sir Isaac Newton

The ability to abstract from and build on the success of others indicates the maturity of any engineering discipline. To date, as witnessed by the limited supply of rather primitive software components from which one can construct new applications, software engineering has not matured as an engineering discipline. Software developers write millions of lines of software each year, yet the average amount of "reuse" is relatively small. The average U.S. reuse ratio is 15.4%, whereas the Japanese reuse ratio is 34.8% [Cus91]. Biggerstaff

---

[1] This material comes from a presentation [Tra92] I was invited to give at the yearly meeting of the Advanced Research Projects Agency (ARPA) Software and Information Systems Office (SISTO) in Los Angeles, April 28–30, 1992. I consider the fact that a riot and fires broke out just after I finished my talk to be a coincidence and not due to the "hot topic" I was addressing.

and Perlis [BP84] and Lanergan and Grasso [LG84] have estimated an attainable reuse ratio of 60% in the scientific application domain, whereas Jones [Jon84] has estimated a reuse potential of 75% to 90% in the business application domain.

This chapter's goal is to identify technical opportunities for researchers to improve the amount of reuse. Table 19.1 lists the most relevant research areas. It is based on the inhibitors identified in the previous chapter. (This table is not meant to be all inclusive, but to serve as an indicator of the wide range of technologies that are necessary to bring the reuse vision expressed a quarter of a century ago [McI69] closer to reality.) The left-hand column of the table contains several reasons often cited for the lack of reuse [Tra87c]. The right-hand column indicates technology that can be applied to overcome the corresponding technical and nontechnical barriers.

Although the title of this chapter might lead the reader to assume that it focuses only on "software" (e.g., code) reuse, current reuse research is focused on a much broader domain of "software artifacts/assets" (e.g., data, processes, test cases, documentation, requirements, designs, and rationale/knowledge). It is important for the reader to avoid dismissing the reuse problem as one of simply developing a subroutine or class library [JF88]. While subroutines, macros, and class libraries clearly exemplify well-known reuse technology, they also result in only meager improvements in quality and productivity (when available).[2] Furthermore, the existence of collections of subroutines or classes in no way guarantees success due to numerous technical and nontechnical inhibitors (e.g., distribution, interface compatibility, parameter/operand compatibility, implementation dependencies, understandability, licensing requirements, etc.). The most interesting challenges facing reuse researchers today are scaling up reuse to larger size components and the reuse of software components other than code (this includes incorporating reuse earlier in the software development life cycle through the reuse of requirements and designs).

The first section of this chapter provides the reader with a brief review of reuse terminology and approaches. This is followed by a look at conditions necessary for reuse. The final section discusses the technical areas where opportunities exist to improve the amount of software available for reuse and to lead to its subsequent use.

---

[2] There are exceptions to this, of course. In well-architected, narrow domains, subroutine or class libraries have been shown to allow reuse ratios of 80% to 90% (e.g., AT&T and NASA).

Table 19.1: Software Reuse Inhibitors and Technology Facilitators

Reuse Inhibitor	Technology Facilitator
Lack of components to reuse	Domain analysis Knowledge acquisition/representation Standardization of constructs Domain-specific components Multimedia collaboration
Cost to make reusable components	Reengineering environments Prototyping languages and environments Application generator generators
Lack of quality components	Formal specification of interfaces Verification of implementations Standard terminology Compositional optimizers
Can't locate component to reuse	Object-oriented databases Distributed databases High-speed networks Domain taxonomies
Don't understand how to use a component	Design rationale capture Knowledge-based hypermedia Data visualization Algorithm animation
Hard to modify a component	Parameterization Polymorphism Composition constructs
Generalized components too inefficient	Caching Operating systems Extensible languages/compilers Cross-component optimization
Hard to integrate/compose component	Composition/prototyping languages Knowledge capture/manipulation Constraint-based reasoning Layered architectures Tool integration frameworks Verification
Possible intellectual property rights violation	Encryption Authentication Software safety

REUSE REVIEW

Terminology Use or Reuse?

Reuse appears to be a term exclusively (mis)used by the programming profession. No engineering discipline's vocabulary (other than waste water management) refers to the "reuse" or "recycling" of resources. Regardless of whether software developers "use" or "reuse" previously developed software assets, the fact remains that there exist attributes that make certain software artifacts more "reusable" than others. As a minimum, these attributes include [Tra91a] the following:

1. *Usefulness*: The component must provide some useful function.

2. *Usability*: The component must be easy to use (and easy to *understand*).

3. *Quality*: The component and its variations must work.

4. *Adaptability*: (optional) The component must be easy to configure to different contexts (usually through parameterization [Gog89]).

5. *Portability*: (optional) The component must work on different hardware platforms and in different software environments (e.g., operating systems or compilers) (usually through virtual machine interfaces [Par76]).

One can conclude that software researchers who can develop technology to increase the "reusability" of software components will do so by addressing the attributes just listed.[3]

Reuse Approaches: Form or Function

There are two basic approaches [BP84] to reuse: *composition* (a bottom-up approach) and *generation* (a top-down approach). The former deals with software building blocks (e.g., subroutines or Ada packages) that the user glues together. The latter focuses on creating patterns or frameworks that must be filled in (expanded/instantiated) before being used (e.g., macros and application generators).

---

[3] As pointed out in Chapter 1, reuse researchers and the software industry define "reuse" as the use of artifacts that have been designed for reuse. This is contrasted with "salvaged" software that is opportunistically cut and pasted into a new application. The former is planned reuse, the latter is unplanned, ad hoc (or odd-hack) reuse.

There is a natural evolution from a compositional to a generative approach. As one becomes more knowledgeable about applications within a domain, one can identify commonalities within and between implementations. These commonalities first manifest themselves as building blocks in the form of procedural abstractions or abstract data types. With time and experience, one can gain further insights into application designs and recognize a common architectural framework into which the building blocks fit. These architectural frameworks become skeletons or generation templates (frames) that can be filled in either under human (application generator) or computer control (compiler).

The most significant research in the reuse arena has focused on recognizing these reusable components and architectures through domain analysis [Ara89, KCH+90, PD91b, TC92] and the representation and manipulation of the associated knowledge [Bai88, BR91, BO91, BL89, CHSW89, Lub86].

REQUIREMENTS FOR VIABILITY OF REUSE

Industry views software reuse as a means of achieving improvements in programmer productivity and program quality. Yet the reuse of software is the end result of someone having initially recognized, designed, documented, and developed the resource. To facilitate software reuse, one needs to support the process of creating reusable assets and understand the circumstances under which it is viable. Since creating a multiple-point/generalized solution is more costly than creating a specialized, unique solution, one needs to either reduce the cost of creating reusable resources or be assured that the cost of doing so will be recovered, internally, on additional development efforts, or externally through the sale or licensing of reusable assets.

Biggerstaff and Richter [BR87a] cited the following conditions under which reuse previously has been successful in a particular application domain (i.e., numeric computation):

1. a narrow (problem) domain with a small number of abstractions,

2. a well-understood (problem) domain with a standard vocabulary, and

3. a stable (solution) domain with a stable implementation technology.

Based on these observations, one can conclude that, in order to support reuse, one needs technology to isolate implementation technology dependencies (through layering), to establish a standard domain vocabulary (through consensus building), and to support clearly specified, understandable interfaces.

The existence of elaborate library mechanisms to support the search and retrieval of components is not essential. To date, most successful reuse has occurred in application domains consisting of less than 150 "components" [Cus91, HSH+86, Kan86, Mat87]. Furthermore, industry experience has concluded that faceted classification systems [PDF87] are too expensive to support and too complex to maintain, while a relatively simple information retrieval (IR) mechanism gives comparable results with less effort [FG90, FP94].

TECHNOLOGIES THAT FACILITATE REUSE

The following section briefly describes how advances in certain technologies (listed in Table 19.1) could positively affect reuse. Many of these capabilities exist, in some form today, but few are being directly applied to reuse.[4] These technologies roughly fall into two categories: (1) tools and (2) knowledge. Tools assist the user in developing and using reusable resources. Knowledge pertains to process information as well as the broad spectrum of textual and nontextual, explicit and implicit by-products of software development.

The key technologies, where breakthroughs would result in the most significant advances in reuse, are:

- knowledge representation and manipulation and
- software composition (megaprogramming) and optimization of results.

Table 19.2 summarizes the reuse requirements for these applicable technologies.

CONCLUSION

Software reuse is a consensus-building activity. By using a previously developed software artifact, one accepts a standard set by others. Similarly, by using a previously developed software artifact, one copies the intellectual effort of another. This chapter has identified technology to support the development of reusable software components as well as to provide economic incentives to do so by protecting the intellectual property rights of the developers.

---

[4] The following analysis is not meant to be inconclusive. Overlaps exist in the technologies and associated requirements, which are subject to personal interpretation and eventual refinement.

Table 19.2: Software Reuse Technology Requirements

Technology	Reuse Requirements
Domain analysis	1. Identification of reusable resources. 2. Providing search and classification context. 3. Providing design rationale. 4. Providing context for understanding software.
Knowledge acquisition, representation, and manipulation	1. Representation of constraints, requirements, and semantics of components and relationships between components. 2. Manipulation of knowledge by tools in the environment to assist the user in locating, configuring, integrating and understanding artifacts. 3. Manipulation and application of encoded process knowledge. *Note*: Knowledge acquisition is very similar to the domain analysis process.
Standardization	1. Consensus building capability through cooperative computing. 2. Issue-based multiuser communication protocols. 3. Families of components with standard interfaces and functional semantics.
Components	1. Libraries of parameterized components targeted for various computer platforms, languages, operating systems, etc.
Reengineering	1. (Semi)automated design recovery, data flow, control flow, and dependency analysis to support reverse engineering. 2. Forward engineering capabilities to trace or transform requirements into implementations (using domain-specific knowledge) to various computer processor and bus architecture configurations (portability).
Prototyping	1. Ability to specify operational and behavioral semantics of software architectures and components. 2. Ability to model and analyze software system configurations consisting of existing implementations and prototyped modules targeted to various computer processor and bus architecture configurations. 3. Ability to prototype systems with multilingual components.

Table 19.2: Continued

Technology	Reuse Requirements
Application generator generators	1. Extend compiler generator technology. 2. Provide construction and debug capability at higher level than source code. 3. Support testability of generators.
Formal methods	1. The ability to formally specify the semantics of modules to facilitate understanding and validation of requirements. 2. Facilitate verification of adaptations of modules through parameterization and composition. 3. Facilitate verification of module implementations. 4. In a layered architecture, facilitate verification of properties preserved across instantiations of layers.
Compositional optimizers	1. Define component composition mechanisms based on control-flow and data-flow constructs targeted for heterogeneous and homogeneous computer configurations. 2. Provide optimization of parameterized components within and across module boundaries. *Note*: Compositional constructs may be viewed as part of the prototyping technology research venue.
Object-oriented databases	1. Facilitate storing of software components, architectures, rationale, relationships, designs, requirements, etc. 2. Provide access control when necessary. 3. Provide storage and manipulation of nontextual information (graphics, audio, and video).
Distributed databases	1. Support large multidomain-specific collections of software components.
High-speed networks	1. Facilitate software component interchange and associated large bodies of textual and nontextual knowledge.
Domain taxonomies	1. Assist in the standardization and classification of knowledge. 2. Facilitate searching for components.
Design rationale capture	1. Support the capture and manipulation of issues, alternatives, options, and arguments.
Hypermedia	1. Support the mapping and navigation of textual and nontextual software artifacts.

Table 19.2: Continued

Technology	Reuse Requirements
Data visualization and algorithm animation	1. Support software understanding by offering alternative representations of textual knowledge. *Note*: The possibility of a virtual reality environment might also apply to enhancing software understanding.
Parameterization	1. Parameterization of nonsource code artifacts. 2. Formal specification of parameter semantics. 3. Mechanisms to understand constraints on parameter values and suggest intelligent (valid) defaults. 4. Automate parameterization generation mechanisms based on analysis of similar existing components.
Caching	1. Reduction of run-time overhead due to polymorphism and message passing.
Operating systems	1. Process communication mechanisms.
Extensible languages and compilers	1. Support for the addition of new constructs using mixfix notation. 2. Support for optimization of new constructs.
Constraint-based reasoning	1. Support for verification of composition constructs. 2. Support for verification of instantiation of parameterized components. 3. Support for explanation generation as part of software understanding.
Tool integration frameworks	1. Support for interoperability of data and tools.
Encryption	1. Transmission of trade secrets to authorized clients. 2. Protection of proprietary assets on publicly accessible repositories. 3. Protection of various security level assets.
Authentication	1. Recognition of authorized client (reuser). 2. Recognition of authorized server (reuse provider).
Software safety	1. Creation of parts with certified safety for critical applications. 2. Creation and transmission of virus-free parts.

Chapter 20

The Future

Those who cannot remember the past are condemned to repeat it.

—George Santayana

THE TITLE of this chapter is intentionally vague—as the future often is. By design, this chapter strives to wrap up some loose ends and give the reader a plan by which their future could best be served through the successful institutionalizing of a reuse program in their organization. By intent, this chapter speculates on the future directions of the state of the art and state of the practice of software reuse. Finally, by the "bye,"[1] this chapter ends with a final confession.

But first, this chapter takes a step backward before looking forward by reviewing the key issues surrounding institutionalizing software reuse. This is followed by a discussion of a "reuse maturity model," which can serve as a framework for assessing the gap between an organization's current reuse practices and their reuse potential.

The chapter closes by reviewing the "Requirements" identified in the first chapter as being necessary for successfully institutionalizing software reuse:

1. getting top *management* support,

2. modifying the software development *process*,

3. overcoming *nontechnical* inhibitors,

4. creating *incentive programs* (carrot and stick),

5. establishing reuse *measurements*,

---

[1] Sorry, couldn't resist a "closing" pun.

6. developing reuse *guidelines*, and

7. focusing on a *single domain*.

REUSE LESSONS LEARNED

This book has addressed several key issues regarding software reuse. By way of review, the following four subsections summarize and analyze the opinions of other reuse experts.[2]

The first section looks at why reuse projects fail, as offered by Ruben Prieto-Díaz. The second section discusses when reuse works, from the perspective of Ted Biggerstaff. The next section, on the realities of reuse, contains a collection of observations made by Ruben Prieto-Díaz and others. The last section presents an overview of the key elements of the DoD reuse initiative vision/strategy.

Why Reuse Projects Fail

Ruben Prieto-Díaz [PD91a] offered the following reasons "Why reuse projects fail":

1. Lack of *management* support for a reuse program.

2. No *incentives* to develop reusable software, or to use it.

3. No procedures or *processes* in place that address reuse issues.

4. Not enough *information* in catalog (no critical mass).

5. Poor *classification* to find components.

6. No automated *library* to support and control reuse.

7. Poor *interfaces* in the components put in the library.

8. The original parts not *designed for reuse*.

---

[2] Each of the first three subsections summarizes statements made by a reuse expert during a panel session at the 13th International Conference on Software Engineering, May 1990, in Austin, Texas [Fra91]. This is followed by some commentary and interpretation of their remarks. I have tried to be objective in interpreting each expert's remarks. In the ideal case, there would be an opportunity for rebuttal. Maybe future editions of this book will include just that.

Analysis. In comparing this list to the "Requirements" list given in the preceding section, one can see clear agreement on points 1 (management), 2 (incentives), and 3 (process). The last two items: 7 (interface design) and 8 (design for reuse) concur with the sixth item on the "Requirements" list (reuse guidelines). That leaves the middle three items, 4 (critical mass), 5 (classification), and 6 (library support), not explicitly called out in the "Requirements" list. The importance of "critical mass" is reflected in the last "Requirement" (focusing on a single domain). One can argue that by focusing on a single domain, one does not dilute one's resources to the point where a critical mass is not available to make the modifications to the development process worthwhile nor does it motivate software developers to design for/look for components to reuse.

The remaining two items (classification and library support) reflect Ruben's thesis work [PD85] on faceted classification and his recent work in domain analysis [PD87, PDA91, PD91b]. Whereas, in my opinion, it is clear that a simple database under proper configuration management is all that is needed to institutionalize reuse (when one focuses on a single domain), there are more ambitious situations when a more sophisticated library system may be of some utility. In this case, several commercially and publicly available reuse library mechanisms are available for use.

Finally, I agree with Ruben on the importance of classification, not from the perspective of creating facets for software component storage, search, and retrieval, but from the domain analysis perspective. That is, establishing a domain ontology and taxonomy is necessary to properly model a domain before it is populated with reusable components.

When Reuse Works

Ted Biggerstaff [Big91], in his position statement, observed that reuse is successful:

1. in narrow domains,

2. in well-understood domains/architectures,

3. when domain knowledge changes slowly,

4. when intercomponent standards exist,

5. when economies of scale to market apply (lots of projects to amortize cost), and

6. when economies of scale in technologies apply (large components are available with large payoffs).

Analysis. Clearly the first item on this list coincides with the last "Requirement" (single domain). Similarly, the last two items (potential number of uses and size of the components) indirectly fall out from focusing on a single domain and the first "Requirement" (getting management support). That is, when one presents a business case to management in order to secure the necessary resources to create reusable assets in a particular domain, normally part of one's justification is an estimate of the return on investment (ROI), based on some number of potential (re)uses.

Finally, item 4 (intercomponent communication) reflects the importance of the reuse guidelines "Requirement" (a form of interface design). In addition, the remaining items, 2 and 3 (well-understood and stable domains), offer insight into design for reuse techniques as reflected in the second software reuse "Rules of Thumb," which were identified in Chapter 1.

1. One should separate *context* from *content* and *concept* and

2. factor out *commonality*, or rephrasing this second rule, isolate *change*.

The Realities of Reuse

Ruben Prieto-Díaz concluded his position paper at ICSE-13 by making the following observations:

1. Reuse is more effective in narrow, well-understood domains.

2. Technology is important, but not essential for reuse.

3. Infrastructure support is essential for reuse.

4. Software reuse requires a change in the software development process.

5. A reuse library is a support tool, not a goal of a reuse program.

6. Classification is instrumental in domain understanding.

In addition, Toshiba's Kazuo Matsumura hit the reuse nail on the head nicely when he said [Mat91]:

"Reuse is a long-term solution that requires an investment."

Analysis. The quote by Matsumura emphasizes the first "Requirement" of getting management support to develop reusable assets in a particular domain. The first item in Ruben's list (narrow domains) coincides with the last "Requirement" (a single domain). The second item (technology) indirectly acknowledges the third "Requirement" of overcoming the nontechnical inhibitors. The third item (infrastructure) may be interpreted as part of the last three "Requirements" (incentives, measurements, and guidelines), because these are all (nontechnical) infrastructure issues in setting up a reuse program. The fourth item (process) cannot be overstated as a "Requirement."

Finally, the last two items (libraries and classification) are nicely put into perspective as to the roles they play in creating a reuse environment and process.

DoD Reuse Initiative Vision/Strategy

The DoD Reuse Executive Steering Committee, led by Jim Hess, has developed a reuse strategy [Pip92] consisting of the following 10 steps:

1. Establish domains.

2. Define reusable products.

3. Establish criteria for deciding ownership.

4. Integrate reuse into the development and maintenance process.

5. Define a model for business decisions.

6. Define metrics to evaluate reuse success.

7. Define component guidelines.

8. Identify technology base.

9. Provide education and training.

10. Provide near-term products and services.

Analysis. These 10 steps may be interpreted as the DoD's road map to institutionalizing software reuse. Every item in the "Requirements" list is addressed, to some extent, by this strategy. In particular the domain, process, measurements, and guidelines "Requirements" map into items 1/2/8, 4, 6, and 7, respectively. Items 3 (ownership), 5 (business model), and 10 (support) address management issues. Finally, item 8 (education) can arguably be labeled as overcoming nontechnical inhibitors. This strategy, coupled with the NIST Component-Based Initiative described in Chapter 1 [Fis94], signals an encouraging change in the government's posture toward developing reusable software assets and nurturing a component-based software industry.

REUSE MATURITY MODEL

Determining how much of an effort it will take to institutionalize software reuse in one's organization depends on one's current software development processes and practices as well as the type of application domain being considered. Several reuse maturity models have been suggested (e.g., Harris [KH91], STARS [Dav92], SPC [DW92, Dav93], HP, IBM, and Loral Federal Systems). Each has five "levels" and has been motivated by the *SEI Capability Maturity Model* [PCC91], which identifies the following five levels of software development maturity:

1. *Initial:* (ad hoc) chaotic process.

2. *Repeatable:* (intuitive) individualistic process.

3. *Defined:* (qualitative) defined process.

4. *Managed:* (quantified) measured process.

5. *Optimizing:* (evolving) feedback improvement process.

The five levels in the Harris and IBM reuse maturity models summarized next are the same (the IBM model being derived from the Harris model). These five levels are:

1. *Initial or chaotic:* uncoordinated reuse efforts.

2. *Monitored:* management awareness of reuse but not the focus.

3. *Coordinated:* reuse is encouraged but there is no investment.

4. *Planned:* organizational support for reuse exists.

5. *Ingrained:* reuse is institutionalized.

As each level of reuse is reached, certain "capabilities" are exhibited in different areas. As indicated by the preceding list, as the maturity level increases, so does the level of management commitment. Another dimension is the scope of reuse. For example, reuse starts off as a individual activity (level 1), becomes a small group activity (level 2), involves the entire department (level 3), is supported by the project or site (level 4), and becomes enterprise-wide (level 5). In other areas such as tools, the following road map might exist: no library (level 1), an informal, unsupervised database (level 2), a database with configuration management and component documentation requirements (level 3), a supported reuse repository with check-out and check-in mechanisms (level 4), and a collection of domain-specific reuse libraries (level 5).

The last example of different levels of maturity in reuse focuses on the types of components being used. For example, subroutines and macros (level 1), modules and packages (level 2), subsystems, patterns/frameworks (level 3), application generators (level 4), and domain-specific software architectures (architecture description and software composition languages) (level 5).

One criticism of such maturity rating systems is that organizations may be at a level 3 in five out of six categories, and at a level 1 in the other category, resulting in no clear rating indicative of their true capability. Furthermore, the reuse ratios in that organization may be higher than those in an organization that is evaluated at the fourth level due, in part, to the nature of the domain, the personalities of the employees, and the company culture. This is why some practitioners recommend that the reuse maturity/capability models be used as frameworks or growth paths for organizations to use to derive their own reuse strategy.

Another maturity model is one proposed by Loral Federal Systems. Their five-level model reflects an initial emphasis on process for the first three levels, then an emphasis on the types of components being reused.

1. *Initial:* ad hoc process.

2. *Basic:* defined process at the project level.

3. *Systematic:* standard process at the site level.

4. *Domain oriented:* large-scale reuse of subsystems.

5. *Software manufacturing:* configurable generators and DSSAs.

Finally, Table 20.1, developed by Martin Griss at Hewlett-Packard, shows the different reuse "maturity" levels with associated reuse ratios and

Table 20.1: Griss's Levels of Software Reuse

Maturity Level	Reuse Ratio	Requirements
No reuse	−20% to +20%	Business as usual Smart people
Salvaging	10% to 50%	Smart people Depends on luck Maintenance problems
Planned reuse	30% to 40%	Reuse library Management support Incentives
Systematic reuse	50% to 70%	Reuse library Reuse process Reuse metrics Education
Domain-oriented reuse	80% to 90%	Domain analysis Application generators Architectures

requirements. It's interesting to note that at the lowest level, a negative reuse ratio (−20%) can be recorded. This occurs when there is duplicity of effort within organizations (e.g., reinventing wheels).

INSTITUTIONALIZING SOFTWARE REUSE

The first chapter identified seven "requirements" for successfully institutionalizing software reuse.

The sections that follow offer some additional insight into these issues and how they may be addressed to achieve the goal of institutionalizing software reuse.

1. Getting Top Management Support

Management needs to be convinced that software reuse is a worthwhile investment. To achieve this goal, software organizations can do the following:

- Point out companies where reuse has been successful (e.g., Schlumberger [ASP93], HP [Gri93a], and Celcius [Mos93]).

- Develop a business case showing long-term paybacks from the initial investment [PCH93]. This may involve starting a pilot project.[3]

- Assess the competition's reuse initiatives to determine if one can remain competitive without embracing reuse.

- Develop a case study including a risk assessment pertaining to the loss of corporate knowledge and experience/expertise due to employee turn-over that otherwise could not be leveraged without it being captured as part of the domain analysis process associated with software reuse.

Without top management support, there is no motivation for change. More importantly, without top management support, there is no money to establish the necessary infrastructure and critical mass of software artifacts.

For a more in-depth treatment of software reuse management issues, see [GFP93].

2. Modifying the Software Development Process

Chapter 1 described how software reuse could be introduced into the various stages in the software development life cycle. The real question for the reader becomes "Does your organization have a process to modify?" Finally, one should note the obvious dependency between modifying the software development process and establishing reuse guidelines (Step 5).

3. Overcoming Nontechnical Inhibitors

Chapters 7 and 18 provided detailed treatment of the types of excuses/inhibitors that have to be overcome in order to institutionalize reuse successfully. The following list summarizes the key issues:

1. *The WIMP syndrome:* As pointed out in Chapter 6, the world is full of well-intentioned but mediocre programmers. One important reason for management's involvement in setting up a reuse program is to overcome this negative inertia.

2. *The will problem:* Associated with the WIMP syndrome is a class of individuals who will not change unless they are told that they *will do it.*

---

[3] For information on setting up a reuse pilot project/program, see [GFP93].

For these individuals, a stick is better than a carrot as a way of effecting change.

3. *The chicken and the egg:* Who will provide/pay for the artifacts that will be reused? This is a difficult question to answer without having some success in small domains on which to draw.

4. *Tools and training:* Finally, a well-thought-out training program for programmers *and* management is necessary in order to change an organization's corporate culture to embrace reuse.

4. Creating Incentive Programs

There are different types of incentive programs. These can be characterized as being the proverbial "carrot" or "stick."

As a "carrot" type of incentive, reuse programs at IBM, Bell Labs, GTE, Hitachi, and Hartford Insurance Company have used financial or token symbolic awards to motivate their employees to participate in their reuse programs. Most of the time these award programs are temporary and intended as a technology insertion aide [Pou95]. They typically reward the developer of the reusable component by associating some cost savings for each time a component is used. Similarly, some (but not all) organizations reward the reuser for cost avoidance in not writing the software from scratch.

The second form of incentive is the "stick." Here, reuse ratios (i.e., how much software in an application is reused rather than written new) and deposition ratios (how much software per delivered lines of code was made reusable and placed in the reuse library) are set and become an evaluation criterion or condition for employment/competition on a contract.

5. Establishing Reuse Measurements

Ultimately, the institutionalization of software reuse must lead to some measured improvement in development cost, schedule, and/or quality. Without a strong software metrics program in place, there is no way to tell if reuse is having any impact.

One of the traditional problems facing the software development community is the long-standing misunderstanding of the term *software reuse*. As pointed out in Chapter 1, software developers in the past grouped many forms of reuse together (e.g., carry-over code, salvaged code, ported code, etc.). The consensus definition of *reusable software* is software that was designed to be reused.[4] By taking this stricter interpretation, one can better apply economic models [GD89, PCH93] to predict schedule and cost savings from reuse. Furthermore one can apply a different set of cost factors to the other forms of reuse, thus getting a more accurate prediction of development costs.

Reuse measures currently in use include the following:

1. *Reuse ratio:* the percentage of reused code in the entire application.

2. *Deposition ratio:* the percentage of developed code that is made reusable.

3. *Reuse utility factor:* a formula that takes into account the size and number of uses of a component. The rationale for this metric is that there are two factors in determining a reusable component's value: how many times it is reused and how much code didn't have to be written. The bigger the utility, the more savings achieved.

An additional dilemma in setting up a reuse program is determining what to count. This is especially critical when incentive programs are associated with a reuse program. Whether one counts the first call or every call to a reused component, the first expansion of a macro, or every expansion of a macro, can lead to conservative or unrealistic reuse percentages. That is why some reuse programs view reuse as "good programming style" and take a more conservative view of only counting the expanded code once.

See "The Business Case for Software Reuse" [PCH93] for an in-depth look into reuse metrics.

6. Developing Reuse Guidelines

Training is essential for the transition of any new technology. Because reuse requires a certain discipline in design and documentation to assure that a software component's domain of applicability is adequately defined, reuse guidelines and standards must be in place in order to populate the reuse library with the kinds of components that are useful and usable. Guidelines for developing reusable components are a good place to start, but several additional guideline documents are necessary in order to institutionalize a reuse program.

---

[4] Some organizations place an additional restriction that the software must come from a "supported" reuse library (i.e., the components are maintained by an outside organization).

For example, the IBM Corporate Reuse Center funded the development of a suite of guideline documents. These documents addressed the following topics:

1. How to Design Software for Reuse,

2. How to Design Software with Reusable Components,

3. How to Set Up and Run a Reuse Program,

4. Software Reuse Legal Issues,

5. Domain Analysis,

6. Reuse Incentive Programs,

7. Software Reuse Operating Procedures, and

8. Software Repository Management Issues.

As an additional reference, the Software Productivity Consortium in Reston, Virginia, has developed an extensive set of guidelines. In particular, the *Reuse Adoption Guidebook* [SPC93] "supports organizations in the definition, evolution, and implementation of reuse programs" [Dav94].

7. Focusing on a Single Domain

There are two types of domain analysis: horizontal and vertical. *Horizontal domain analysis* focuses on identifying functional commonality across application domains. *Vertical domain analysis* concentrates on identifying functional commonality within an application domain, for a family of applications within that domain.

Examples of software components that are reusable across domains are graphical user interface modules, data structures, basic communications packages, and utilities. Although there is an increased chance for a larger ROI for developing these types of reusable resources (or buying them off the shelf), experience shows that the average application[5] bottoms out at a reuse ratio of 20% to 25%. That is, one can construct less than half of any given application from domain-independent reusable components. This is clearly an improvement, but far from the 80% to 90% reuse ratios often cited [Jon84, Bas87, LG84].

---

[5] If there ever was such a thing as an "average" application.

To get higher levels of reuse (and correspondingly higher improvements in productivity), one needs to focus on developing domain-specific reusable artifacts. This is the emphasis of the ARPA-sponsored Domain-Specific Software Architecture program with demonstration projects by Loral (avionics domain) [TC93b], Teknowledge (integrated logistics), and Honeywell (navigation and guidance domain). In addition, great success has been demonstrated at Hewlett Packard with their "Kits" [Gri93b, GW94] and at Schlumberger with their "Technology Books" [ASP93].

CLOSING CONFESSION

By now you are probably fed up with the pun-ishment you have been bombarded with throughout this book. Whether there will be more "Confessions" is an unanswerable question. I would think "When will there be . . ." is a more appropriate question to pose. The answer depends on what kind of hand the fickle finger of fate deals me and what kind of warped mood it leaves me in. Until then, keep those keyboards clicking and why not get a library card to your favorite reuse repository and check out what they have on their shelves? You may be in for a surprise! But then again, maybe you would rather spend a week programming to save you the five minutes browsing in the library.

In looking at software reuse for the last few years, I have gone through several phases.

1. *Blind enthusiasm:* that there are potential improvements in quality and productivity.

2. *Bitter resentment:* that nontechnical issues seem to inhibit its progress.

3. *Painful disillusion:* that there was nothing "new" about software reuse.

4. Finally, *guarded optimism:* that there is a light at the end of the tunnel; that new technologies exist that will support software reuse.

In closing, I would like to leave you with one of my favorite bits of humor.

It seems there was this man walking through the woods. He saw a boy leaning up against a tree with a stopwatch in his hand and an apple on his head. The man said, "What are you doing with an apple on your head and a stopwatch in your hand?" "Time will tell!" the boy answered.

So, time will tell if the information found in this book will help you avoid the potholes and tar pits along the arduous path to institutionalizing software reuse. I wish you the best as you set off on the journey.

WHERE TO FIND MORE (FREE) INFORMATION

Several good reuse resources are available to the interested internet surfer. The results of the last three Workshops on Institutionalizing Software Reuse (WISR), including working group summaries, are available on-line. In addition, there is one reuse related news group and at least two reuse electronic distribution lists one can join. Directions for accessing these resources are as follows:

- Workshop on Institutionalizing Software Reuse Proceedings: FTP to gandalf.umcs.maine.edu and look in the /pub/WISR/wisrn directory, where "n" is the workshop number.
- Reuse Education and Training Workshop Proceedings: Available in the ASSET Repository (contact info@source.asset.com).
- Reuse mailing list: To subscribe, send a request to listserv@wunet.wustl.edu asking to subscribe to *reuse* or *reusewg*.
- Reuse News Group: Read comp.sw.components on usenet.

These resources represent just the tip of the iceberg. Once you are plugged into the reuse mainstream, you can drink your fill of reuse tidbits and techniques.

Finally, for those ready to cruise the information highway in style, check out the world wide web/mosaic reuse home page at the University of Houston at Clear Lake by David Eichmann:

http://rbse.jsc.nasa.gov/eichmann/rbse.html

the ADAGE (Avionics Domain Application Generation Environment) DSSA home page:

http://www.ai.mit.edu/projects/adage/adage.html

or the STARS (Software Technology for Adaptable Reliable Systems) home page:

http://www.stars.ballston.paramax.com/index.html

WHERE TO FIND MORE REUSE INFORMATION

If you are so moved to go to your favorite university or company library, you may be able to find one of the following to satisfy your thirst for reuse knowledge. Look for the following software reuse books and reports:

- *Software Reuse: Emerging Technology*, by Will Tracz. Published by IEEE Computer Society Press, 1988.

- *Software Reusability*, edited by Ted Biggerstaff and Alan Perlis. Published by Addison-Wesley and ACM Press, 1989.

- *Software Reuse Guidelines and Methods*, by James Hooper and Rowena Chester. Published by Plenum Publishing, 1991.

- *Software Reusability*, edited by W. Shaefer, R. Prieto-Díaz, and M. Matsumoto. Published by Ellis Horwood, Chichester, 1993.

- *WISR '92, Fifth Annual Workshop on Software Reuse Summary and Working Group Reports*, edited by Martin Griss and Will Tracz. Published in *ACM Software Engineering Notes*, April 1993, Vol. 18, No. 2, pp. 74–85.

- *Second International Workshop on Software Reusability Summary*, by Will Tracz. Published in *ACM Software Engineering Notes*, July 1993.

- *Proceedings of IWSR '93*. Published by IEEE Computer Society Press, 1993.

- *WISR '93, Sixth Annual Workshop on Software Reuse Summary and Working Group Reports*, edited by Jeff Poulin and Will Tracz. Published in *ACM Software Engineering Notes*, January 1994, Vol. 19, No. 1, pp. 55–71.

- *Success Factors of Systematic Reuse*, edited by W. B. Frakes and Sadahiro Isoda. Special issue on software reuse. Published in *IEEE Software*, September 1994.

The following are domain analysis books and reports:

- *Domain Analysis*, by Ruben Prieto-Díaz. Published by IEEE Computer Society Press, 1991.

- *Reuse Library Process Model*, by Ruben Prieto-Díaz. STARS CDRL 03041-002, July 1991.

- *Domain Analysis Guidelines*, by W. C. Vitaletti and R. Chhut. SofTech, Inc., May 1992.

- *A Domain Analysis Process*, by A. Jawarski, F. Hills, T. Durek, S. Faulk, and J. Gaffney. Software Productivity Consortium, January 1990.

- *A Domain Analysis Bibliography*, by J. A. Hess, et al. CMU/SEI-90-SR-3, June 1990.

- *Feature-Oriented Domain Analysis (FODA)*, by K. C. Kang et al. CMU/SEI-90-TR-21, November 1990.

- *Domain Analysis Working Group Report*, by Will Tracz. Published in *ACM Software Engineering Notes*, July 1992.

- "DSSA Frequently Asked Questions," in *ACM Software Engineering Notes*, April 1994, Vol. 19, No. 2, pp. 52–56.

Appendix A

Domain-Specific Software Architecture Engineering Process Guidelines

ONE OF the dilemmas that has prevented software developers from re-using software is the lack of software artifacts to use or the existence of artifacts that are difficult to integrate. Domain-specific software architectures (DSSAs) have been proposed [Met90] in order to address these issues. A DSSA not only provides a framework for reusable software components to fit into, but captures the design rationale and provides for a degree of adaptability. This appendix presents process guidelines for defining a DSSA.[1] Furthermore, the process is formally specified in the Teamware Process Programming Language [YT92].

INTRODUCTION

The material that follows defines a *domain-engineering process*[2] to be used to generate a DSSA. It is based on the *Reuse Library Process Model* that was developed as part of the STARS (Software Technology for Adaptable and Reliable Systems) program by Ruben Prieto-Díaz [PD91b] and the *Feature-Oriented Domain Analysis (FODA)* work by Kang et al. [KCH+90] at the Software Engineering Institute (SEI) cast into the methodology supported by the

---

[1]This effort is sponsored by the U.S. Department of Defense Advanced Research Projects Agency in cooperation with the U.S. Air Force Wright Laboratory Avionics Directorate under contract F33615-91-C-1788. I also would like to acknowledge Lou Coglianese and Steve Shafer for their many contributions to this material.

[2]*Note*: A process is a series of steps or stages with entry and exit criteria and tasks to follow at each phase as well as a way of verifying its correctness and merit.

Requirements Driven Design tool (RDD-100[3]) [Cor91] and the Issue Based Information Systems [KR79] (IBIS) model for recording design decisions and design rationales.

The fundamental premises of this work are that

1. an application can be defined by a set of needs that it fulfills,

2. user needs can be translated into a set of requirements that meet those needs,

3. requirements can be met in a number of different ways (multiple solutions), and

4. implementation constraints limit the number of ways requirements can be met.

The goal of the process is to map user needs into system and software requirements that, based on a set of implementation constraints, define a DSSA.

The separation of user needs from system requirements and implementation constraints differentiates this process from previous work. In particular most domain analysis processes do not differentiate between *functional requirements* and *implementation constraints*, but rather simply classify them under the heading of "requirements." This differentiation distinguishes other "domain analysis" processes from the "domain engineering" process described in this appendix. Existing domain analysis processes fail to distinctly separate "problem domain analysis" from "solution space analysis." In particular, they tend to focus on the latter rather than the former.[4] Domain-modeling processes (e.g., the OCU model [Lea88]), on the other hand, focus on problem domain analysis. The domain engineering process described in this appendix addresses the issues raised by both domain modeling and domain analysis processes in the definition of a DSSA:

> A domain-specific software architecture is, in effect, a multiple-point solution to a set of application-specific requirements (which define a problem domain).

Another difference between this approach to domain engineering and other domain analysis approaches (e.g., Prieto-Díaz [PD87]) is that case-based

---

[3]RDD-100 is a registered trademark of the Ascent Logic Corporation.

[4]Although their authors would probably find this to be a good point of discussion!

reasoning and reverse engineering are *not* central mechanisms for identifying reusable resources, but rather existing applications are used as vehicles to validate the architectures that are derived, top-down, from generalized user requirements. The reuse of existing artifacts is not the central goal of the proposed domain engineering process, but rather the goal is the development of a reusable architecture into which well-specified components can be integrated.

At the top-most level there are five stages/phases in the process. Each stage is further divided into steps or substages. Furthermore, this process is concurrent, recursive, and iterative,[5] therefore completion may require several passes through each stage with additional levels of detail being addressed, or new insights (or oversights) requiring further definition or analysis. For example, during *Stage 1, Define the Scope of the Domain*, one concurrently identifies key aspects of the domain, which are part of *Stage 2.5, Create a Domain Vocabulary Dictionary*.

The five stages in the DSSA definition/domain engineering process are:

1. *Define the scope of the domain*: define what can be accomplished—emphasis is on the user's needs.

2. *Define/refine domain-specific elements*: similar to requirements analysis—emphasis is on the problem space.

3. *Define/refine domain-specific design and implementation requirement constraints*: similar to requirements analysis—emphasis is on the solution space.

4. *Develop domain models/architectures*: similar to high-level design—emphasis is on defining module/model interfaces and semantics.

5. *Produce/gather reusable work products*: implementation/collection of reusable artifacts (e.g., code, documentation, etc.).

The remaining material in this appendix focuses on expanding these five stages. Each stage consists of a series of questions to be answered and a list of inputs required, outputs to be generated, and verification criteria. Before each stage is presented in detail, the overall knowledge-acquisition process is discussed and guidelines presented to assist domain engineers in tailoring the process to meet the goals within their specific domain.

---

[5] The process could justifiably be called "spiral."

Finally, included at the end of this appendix is an outline of the STARS Domain Analysis Process [PD91b]. It provides the reader with an opportunity to compare the stages and activities within these two approaches.

Terminology and Definitions

Before proceeding, in order to avoid unnecessary confusion, it is important to alert the reader to the choice of terminology being used to describe this process. The following set of definitions is the result of the DARPA Domain-Specific Software Architecture Workshop in Hidden Valley, Pennsylvania, July 9–12, 1989:

Architecture: 1. A composite or assemblage of models that define the structure or topology of subsystem components, which are defined by a composite of models. 2. A canonical solution to patterns of requirements whose behavior is expressed by the propagation of information among component objects.

Component: 1. An architectural software artifact that can be modeled. 2. An element that may be composed/combined with other elements.

Model: 1. A clearly identifiable interface and description of some design element, module, or object that may be part of a larger model (composed to form) or a separate entity. 2. A scalable unit of engineering technology with known structure and performance that maps function to form. 3. A specification for a class of problems.

Domain-Specific Software Architecture: A context for patterns of problem elements, solution elements, and situations that define mappings between them.

Another interesting result of the workshop was that the attendees resorted to referring to the elements in a DSSA as *"things."* The "things" described by the process in this appendix are classified by the level of abstraction to which they apply and the user who is referring to them. What follows are working definitions of *important terms*, cast in the framework of a software development life cycle. They provide some additional context for the material that follows.

A **customer** talks about his/her problem in terms of what *needs* must be met given certain real *constraints* in creating a solution. The user might want a system with certain *features* or *functional units* that operates a certain way under certain conditions. The customer enters into a contractual relationship with a contractor based on a set of *requirements* that need to be satisfied. These *requirements* detail the constraints (e.g., cost, speed, size, language, hardware platform, etc.) that then must be met by a system that performs the required *functions*.

System engineers (or **requirements analysts**) start off talking about certain *concepts* that exist in a domain. They might build *models* to gain insight into certain aspects of these concepts and how they perform under certain conditions (in certain *contexts*). The system engineer/analyst decomposes the system into hardware and software *elements* or *entities* and assesses certain trade-offs in how these may be realized.

The **programmer/software engineer** designs and builds software *modules* or selects off-the-shelf *components* and tailors them to a particular *context* specific to the task at hand.

The terms *concept, component, module, model, functional unit, element, entity,* and *object* are synonymous to the same "thing," but used differently by different people[6] at different times in the software development life cycle. Special care has been taken throughout this appendix to use them consistently.

Finally, for purposes of clarity, the reader should note that this process makes a special distinction between the term *requirement*, which describes a defining characteristic in the problem space, and the term *constraint*, which describes a discriminating characteristic in the solution space.

RDD-100 Considerations

The RDD-100 (Requirements Driven Design) is a design tool that comes the closest to directly supporting the domain engineering process being described. While its choice of terminology is slightly different than that used in these guidelines, the basic capabilities it provides can be used to record the requirements, design, design alternatives, and rationale. In particular, RDD-100 can be used to create data-flow and control-flow (state-transition) diagrams.

IBIS Implications

One of the most important goals of this domain engineering process is the identification and recording of design decisions, design alternatives, and design

---

[6]*Note*: Historically, the term *concept* is associated with the 3-C Model [Tra91a] (*Concept, Context, and Content*) for designing reusable software components. The term *feature* plays a central role in the FODA process [KCH+90], and *functional units* or *domain entities* are described in the STARS process [PD91b].

rationale. The IBIS (Issue-Based Information Systems) method of recording issues, positions, and arguments provides the foundation for our process:

- *Issues* take the form of a question or decision that needs to be made.

- *Positions* are the possible choices/answers to an issue/question.

- *Arguments* describe why a position is the "right one"—the reasons/rationale (or rule) for making a certain decision.

Obviously, there can be several positions associated with each issue, and several arguments to support each position. Sometimes the same arguments can be used to support other positions.

Tool support is needed when a position is dependent on other issues, for example, "take this position if the position on this issue was X . . . etc." This leads to "connecting issues" into a network that is related either by arguments or positions. Clearly, having the right tools to help record the issues, positions, and arguments can help keep these relationships under control.

By recording domain knowledge in this manner, several things "fall out" for free. In particular, the "decision taxonomy" becomes a collection of the issues that are addressed (positions taken) in some manner.

DSSA DOMAIN ENGINEERING PROCESS OVERVIEW

The proposed domain engineering process consists of the steps that follow. The domain engineer is encouraged to scan this outline and become familiar with the overall structure of the process.

Stage 1: Define the Scope of the Domain Analysis

    Stage 1.1: Define goals of domain analysis

    Stage 1.2: Define the domain

        Stage 1.2.1: Draw a domain diagram

        Stage 1.2.2: Identify scope of domain

        Stage 1.2.3: Identify border of domain

    Stage 1.3: Define domain-specific resources

        Stage 1.3.1: Identify domain experts

        Stage 1.3.2: Identify domain artifacts

Stage 1.4: Define the domain of interest

Stage 1.5: Determine model verification procedure

Stage 2: Define/Refine Domain-Specific Elements

    Stage 2.1: Define/refine an element

        Stage 2.1.1: Identify elements (behavior, temporal, and data) in the domain

        Stage 2.1.2: Identify attributes of elements

            Stage 2.1.2.1: Identify required/essential/mandatory elements

            Stage 2.1.2.2: Identify optional elements

            Stage 2.1.2.3: Identify alternative elements

            Stage 2.1.2.4: Identify requirements common between applications

            Stage 2.1.2.5: Identify requirements that vary between applications

        Stage 2.1.3: Determine element data flow

        Stage 2.1.4: Determine element control flow

        Stage 2.1.5: Identify relationship between elements

            Stage 2.1.5.1: Identify "is a/a kind of" relationships

            Stage 2.1.5.2: Identify "consists of" relationships

            Stage 2.1.5.3: Identify "uses/needs" relationships

    Stage 2.2: Classify elements

    Stage 2.3: Cluster common elements

    Stage 2.4: Create a domain description document

    Stage 2.5: Create a domain vocabulary dictionary

        Stage 2.5.1: Create a domain thesaurus

    Stage 2.6: Create a high-level requirements specification document

    Stage 2.7: Evaluate results and iterate if necessary

Stage 3: Define/Refine Domain-Specific Design and Implementation Requirement Constraints

    Stage 3.1: Define constraints on the architecture

        Stage 3.1.1: Define software constraints

        Stage 3.1.2: Define hardware/physical constraints

        Stage 3.1.3: Define performance constraints

        Stage 3.1.4: Define design constraints

    Stage 3.2: Identify relationships between elements and constraints

Stage 3.3: Evaluate results and iterate if necessary

Stage 4: Develop Domain Architectures/Models

Stage 4.1: Define Domain-Specific Software Architecture(s)

Stage 4.1.1: Define generic high-level design

Stage 4.1.2: Identify components/modules

Stage 4.1.3: Define decision taxonomy

Stage 4.1.4: Record design issues, trade-offs, and decision rationale

Stage 4.2: Define modules

Stage 4.2.1: Define module interface

Stage 4.2.2: Specify semantics of each module

Stage 4.2.3: Specify constraints on each module

Stage 4.2.3.1: Specify performance/timing constraints

Stage 4.2.3.2: Specify dependency (layering) constraints

Stage 4.2.3.3: Specify sequentiality/order (operational) constraints

Stage 4.2.3.4: Specify system design constraints

Stage 4.2.4: Specify performance characteristics of each model

Stage 4.2.5: Identify configuration (generic) parameters for each model

Stage 4.2.6: Record issues, trade-offs, and design rationale

Stage 4.3: Link models to elements and requirements

Stage 4.4: Evaluate results and iterate if necessary

Stage 5: Produce/Gather Reusable Work Products

Stage 5.1: Develop/collect the reusable artifacts

Stage 5.1.1: Identify COTS components

Stage 5.1.2: Identify in-house components

Stage 5.1.3: Determine configurability

Stage 5.1.4: Determine necessary modifications

Stage 5.2: Develop each module

Stage 5.2.1: Implement each module

Stage 5.2.2: Test each module

Stage 5.2.3: Document each module

Stage 5.2.4: Record issues, trade-offs, and design rationale

Stage 5.3: Link artifacts to models, elements, and requirements

PREPARATION FOR APPLYING THE
DOMAIN ENGINEERING PROCESS

What follows is a list of questions to be answered by a domain expert or experts as part of an interview conducted by a domain engineer. It is recommended that the interview process be either video taped or tape recorded so as to allow an unimpeded flow of knowledge not constrained by note-taking. An alternative approach is to have two domain engineers at the interview: one to take notes, the other to ask questions.

Before domain engineers interview domain experts, domain engineers should make every attempt to familiarize themselves with the domain. Ideally the person performing the domain analysis, the domain engineer, has some experience in the domain and this process becomes one of recording the necessary information. The domain engineer should have some idea of the answers to the questions found in these guidelines in order to draw out the answers or have them validated by the domain expert.

Most importantly, the domain engineer should determine which portions of the questions in these guidelines are relevant and modify the domain engineering process accordingly.

It is also important to emphasize that before starting the domain engineering process, the domain engineer should understand what they hope to accomplish and why they are performing this task. Upon completion of the domain engineering process, the domain engineer should have

1. a characterization and understanding of the problem space (the domain),

2. a characterization and understanding of the solution space (for the domain),

3. an understanding of how requirements in the problem space map to solutions within the framework of a generic design (the DSSA), and

4. (optionally) reusable components that can easily be adapted and integrated into the architecture to generate applications within the domain.

To meet this end, the domain engineer must be prepared to ask leading questions such as the following:

- Why is this here?

- What is this?

- Why is it done this way?

- Is there any other way to do it?

Finally, the outputs of the domain engineering process serve several purposes. To facilitate the capture, representation, verification, and navigation of domain-specific knowledge in a knowledge base, a hypertext system is recommended to link various domain elements, requirements, constraints, and components together with supporting documentation (e.g., rationale).

Domain Analysis Time-Line Outline

The following lists the sequence of steps a domain engineer might follow in conducting an initial domain analysis (DA). This schedule has been successfully followed within IBM on several *small* domains by well-trained domain engineers. The reader should be aware that the times may vary, depending on the skills of the domain engineer, the cooperation of the domain experts, and the size of the domain.[7] This outline is offered more as a framework to plan a domain analysis, rather than a hard and fast schedule.

Step 1: Meet with upper management to determine

1. goals of doing the domain analysis and

2. resources (e.g., people, products).
   Time = 1 hour.

Step 2: Contact domain experts and tell them to

1. spend 15 to 45 minutes drawing a high-level block diagram for the design of applications in the domain,

2. identify the major subsystems/modules and the data that flows between them, and

3. be prepared to make a presentation of your diagram at the DA meeting described in the next step.
   Time = 15 minutes × number of domain experts for the domain engineer + 1 hour × number of domain experts.

---

[7] In some cases, an order of magnitude more time might be more realistic than that proposed here! As a general rule of thumb, one labor month per thousand lines of source code is a good estimate.

Step 3: Conduct high-level domain analysis meeting:

1. domain experts present diagrams,

2. identify terminology,

3. clarify elements,

4. work toward consensus at top level, and

5. as time permits, refine drawing to lower levels.
   Time = 4 hours.

Step 4: Domain engineer coalesces knowledge gathered by putting together a strawman:

1. data-flow diagram,

2. dictionary/thesaurus, and

3. issues and trade-offs/rational documents.
   Time = 2–3 days depending on results.

Step 5: Conduct an offline review of results of DA meeting by

1. sending strawmen to domain experts,

2. soliciting their feedback, and

3. having domain engineer rework strawmen based on feedback.
   Time = 2–4 hours/domain expert's time + 2–3 days by domain engineer, depending on type of feedback.

Step 6: Hold second domain analysis (DA) meeting to

1. review results,

2. add detail, and

3. etc. (focus on reason for doing DA, e.g., finding/defining reusable components).
   Time = 8 hours.
   The Domain Engineer would then iterate through Steps 4–6, depending on the resources and goals.

Step 7: Validate results by

1. going through a high-level design review using existing resources to create a new system, or

2. bringing in a domain expert who did not participate in the analysis to review the material for completeness, consistency and accuracy.
   Time = 4–8 hours depending on the size of the domain.

Desirable Attributes of a DSSA

The following is a list of desirable attributes of a DSSA. They serve as goals the domain engineer should keep in mind when conducting the domain engineering process.

- understandability,

- usability,

- complexity (hiding of),

- adaptability,

- configurability,

- extensibility (ability to extend the domain of the DSSA),

- scalability (ability of DSSA to map to implementation of increasing dimension within the domain),

- composability (ability of components to be combined with other components in the DSSA),

- interoperability (ability of components to be integrated with other software not in the DSSA),

- compatibility (with existing standards, terminology, and technology),

- predictability (the level of fidelity of meeting performance and resource requirements),

- quality (of components and supporting documentation), and

- salability (ability of DSSA to reflect the requirements in the eyes of the end user).

Process Diagram Notation

The notation used in the process diagrams that follow has been developed as part of the Teamware Process Programming Language [YT92]. Teamware has been designed to support both specification and enactment of software processes.

Figure A.1 shows some simple Teamware diagrams. Flow of control between activities is shown by using the four connectors: ■ (fork processes),

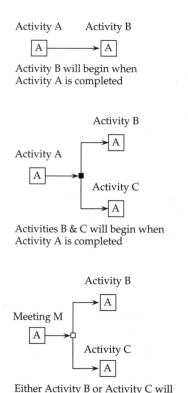

Activity A   Activity B

Activity B will begin when
Activity A is completed

Activity B

Activity A

Activity C

Activities B & C will begin when
Activity A is completed

Activity B

Meeting M

Activity C

Either Activity B or Activity C will
begin when Meeting M is completed

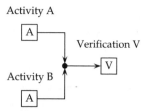

Activity A

Verification V

Activity B

Verification Activity V will begin when both
Activity A and Activity B have been completed

Activity A

Activity C

Activity B

Activity C will begin when either
Activity A or Activity B has been completed

Multiple Activity A

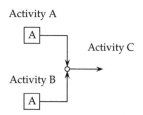

Multiple instances of a given activity will be carried
out in parallel (e.g., execute multiple Code-Module
activities, one for each module in the system)

Figure A.1:   Some Simple Teamware Examples

● (join forked processes), □ (alternative paths), and ○ (join alternative paths). During execution, Teamware interpreter handles activities differently depending on their system specification. For example, meeting activities are interpreted differently from general assigned activities. The letters in the activity boxes denote the activity's system specification. In the domain engineering process we will differentiate between general assigned activities (labeled *A*) and verification activities (labeled *V*).

STAGE 1: DEFINE THE SCOPE OF THE DOMAIN ANALYSIS

The first phase in the domain engineering process focuses on determining what is in the domain of interest and to what ends this process is being applied. One of the primary outputs of this phase is a list of needs that users of applications in this domain require to be met.

The answers to the first set of questions that follow should be determined by the interviewer before the first interview commences. In that way, the interviewer is better prepared to take advantage of the first working session to ask the domain expert to verify these answers. Similarly, the answers to as many of the questions in the remaining portion of this section should be determined beforehand so that the domain expert can validate or expand on them.

1. What is the name of the domain being modeled?

2. What is a short description of the application domain?

3. What general user needs are satisfied by applications in this domain?

Figure A.2 shows the individual steps in this process stage.

Stage 1.1: Define Goals of Domain Analysis

As with the expression "mileage may vary" used to caution customers regarding published figures on cars, it is important to make the potential user of this domain engineering process aware that the customer's domain analysis "goals may vary."

Domain analysis is done for a variety of reasons. Although creating a DSSA is the major emphasis of this process, other applications of the process are equally relevant. The Workshop on Domain Modeling at ICSE-13 in Austin, Texas, May 13, 1991, identified the following applications for domain analysis:

1. understanding large systems as a maintenance aide,

2. translation of natural language test scripts for mechanical testing,

3. evolution of software design,

4. classification of software components, and

5. developing specification languages and synthesizers.

In addition, at the First International Workshop on Software Reuse in Dortmund, Germany, July 3–5, 1991, the Domain Analysis Working Group observed domain analysis being applied at various phases in the software life cycle for the following reasons:

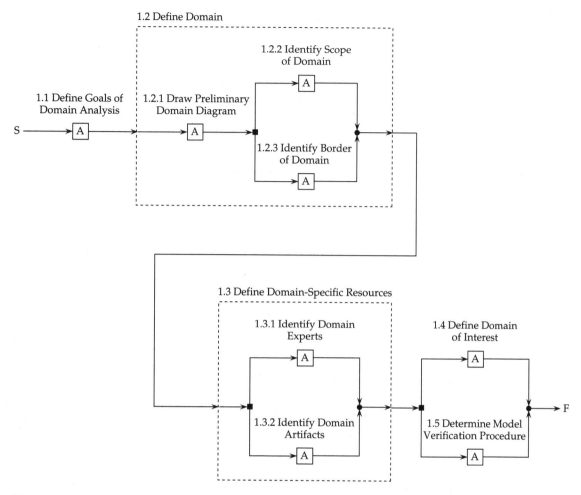

Figure A.2: Stage 1: Define the Scope of the Domain Analysis

1. *Product definition*: Domain analysis can be used prior to product development to determine what people want.

2. *Requirements analysis*: Domain analysis can be used to analyze the characteristics of the application domain and cite opportunities for software reuse of common modules.

3. *Design*: Domain analysis techniques can help with the design of software for reuse by understanding what the domain of applicability/configurability is that should be addressed.

4. *Maintenance*: Reverse engineering, as a form of domain analysis, can lead to the identification and classification of software components that can be reused.

5. *Implementation*: Creating new applications with reusable software components, integrating components on a generic architecture, or generating new applications through parameter selection are approaches that are feasible as a result of domain analysis.

Questions relevant to defining the goals of the domain engineering are:

1. What is the purpose of creating this DSSA?

2. What is the DSSA going to be used for?

3. Who is going to use the DSSA?

4. When do you know you are done doing a domain analysis?

5. What are the reuse goals? How much of the architecture should be reusable?

Stage 1.2: Define the Domain

The goal of this stage in the domain engineering process is to draw a high-level block diagram showing what is in the domain and the relationships between the entities in the domain (e.g., an E/R diagram).

Stage 1.2.1: Draw Preliminary Domain Diagram

Identify what is inside the scope of this domain analysis. Assuming a block diagram has been drawn, this step labels the blocks and makes the first attempt at identifying variations.

1. What are the classes of applications in this domain?

2. What primary *functions/objects/things* are in the domain?

3. What kinds of (high-level) trade-offs exist in this domain?

Stage 1.2.2: Identify Scope of Domain

Identify what is outside the scope of this domain analysis. A problem domain generally can be divided into several smaller pieces, or subdomains. These subdomains might share commonality with subdomains in other problem domains (e.g., communication protocol or database acquisition protocols). The focus of this stage is to identify those commonalities and relationships.

1. What functions/objects/things in the domain are outside the scope of the subdomain we are choosing to analyze?

2. What are similar/related domains and subdomains?

3. How does this domain relate to other domains?

Stage 1.2.3: Identify Border of Domain

Identify what is on the borders of the domain. An application generally interacts with other applications either by supplying data or functionality or expecting data or services exported by other resources (e.g., client/server relationships). The focus of this stage is to identify those entities or resources used or supplied and their possible sources or destinations. The domain engineer should pay special attention to the classification of inputs (data/control). This separation will be valuable in later stages of the process.

1. What are the inputs (data/control) to the domain?

2. What are the outputs (data/control) from the domain?

3. Where do inputs to the domain come from (who provides the services/data)?

4. Where do outputs from the domain go to (who consumes the services/data—if known)?

Stage 1.3: Define Domain-Specific Resources

Domain engineers, once their domain analysis goals have been established, must identify the resources from which they can draw on in meeting their goals.

Stage 1.3.1: Identify Domain Experts

Define who you have to work with. The domain engineer must identify the individual or individuals whose expertise and experience in the domain can lend insight into various aspects of the domain, both in defining the requirements for applications in the domain and identifying existing or potential solutions (and their trade-offs).

1. Who (else) knows about the domain under analysis?

2. Who (else) knows about the software implementation details for this domain?

3. Who knows about the system design details for this domain?

4. Who knows about the hardware constraints and dependencies for applications in this domain?

5. Who knows about future user needs for applications in this domain?

6. Who knows about future technology that may be transitioned into new applications in this domain?

Stage 1.3.2: Identify Domain Artifacts

Define what you have to work with. If the reuse of existing software artifacts is one of the primary goals of the domain analysis, then identifying what resources exist is an (obviously) important step. Caution should be exercised when placing excessive dependence on the reverse engineering of existing systems in order to derive a DSSA because of the implementation biases that could exist from analyzing a single-point solution or a family of solutions derived from a single-point solution.

1. What systems exist that reflect the aspects of the type of applications we wish to model?

2. What is the legacy of the systems that exist? How are they the same? How are they different? Why are they different?

3. What relevant documentation exists for existing systems?

4. What textbooks, articles, or models are available that describe applications in this domain?

Stage 1.4: Define Domain of Interest

Once an application domain has been defined, it is not economically feasible to explore all the possible implementation and design trade-offs nor develop all possible implementations in the solution space. Going back to Stage 1.1, *Define Goals of Domain Analysis*, the domain analysis goals should be examined, and based on the results of this stage in the process, a subset of work that could be done should be defined.

1. What applications in this domain are we interested in addressing? (A business decision)

2. What technologies are we interested in using to build applications in this domain? (e.g., OS, language, platform, etc.)

3. Why are certain inputs, outputs, and/or technologies *not* of interest?

4. What methodology are we interested in using to build applications in this domain?

5. What documentation standards are we interested in using to build applications in this domain?

6. How much time and effort is available for the domain engineering effort?

Stage 1.5: Determine Model Verification Procedure

The advantage of having several existing systems as resources from which to draw is that they can be used to validate the resulting DSSA. But this is just one validation mechanism; concurrence regarding the DSSA (and associated artifacts) by domain experts is desirable.

1. What system(s) can be used to validate the correctness of the model(s) and architecture(s)?

2. Who can serve as reviewers for the domain model(s) and architecture(s)?

3. What equipment (simulators/stimulators) is needed to validate the model(s) and architecture(s)?

Stage 1 Inputs

1. Experts (see Stage 1.3.1)

2. Existing systems (see Stage 1.3.2)

3. Existing documentation (e.g., textbooks, articles)

Stage 1 Outputs

1. Block diagram of the domain of interest including inputs and outputs to the domain and high-level relationships between functional units/elements in the domain

2. List of people's names to serve as future references or validation sources

3. List of projects with pointers to documentation and source code

4. List of needs to be met by applications in this domain

Stage 1 Validation Procedure

1. Meet with domain experts to evaluate completeness of information gathered to date. This may take place on several occasions with several different individuals.[8]

2. Meet with end users/customers of applications in this domain to verify that these are the needs they expect applications in this domain to meet.

STAGE 2: DEFINE/REFINE DOMAIN-SPECIFIC ELEMENTS

The goal for this stage in the domain engineering process is to compile a dictionary and thesaurus of domain-specific terminology. Given the high-level block diagram defined in the previous phase of the domain engineering process (Stage 1.2, *Define the Domain*), more detail is added, with special emphasis on *identifying commonalities* and *isolating differences* between applications in the domain. Special emphasis should be placed on trying to "standardize" and "classify" the basic *elements* in the domain.[9] Figure A.3 shows the individual steps in this process stage.

Stage 2.1: Define/Refine an Element

The goal of this stage in the domain engineering process is to add more detail to the block diagram defined in the previous phase by creating data-flow and control-flow (operational sequences or state-transition) diagrams.

---

[8]*Note*: Just as "beauty is in the eye of the beholder," the "correctness" of the domain engineering results may be subject to the opinion of the domain expert. Therefore, the domain engineer is urged to exercise diplomacy in resolving conflicting expert testimony.

[9]*Note*: The basic elements in the domain are also referred to as *entities* or *concepts*. In MIL-STD-499B they are referred to as *primary functions*. See the discussion earlier in this chapter for an additional discussion of this topic.

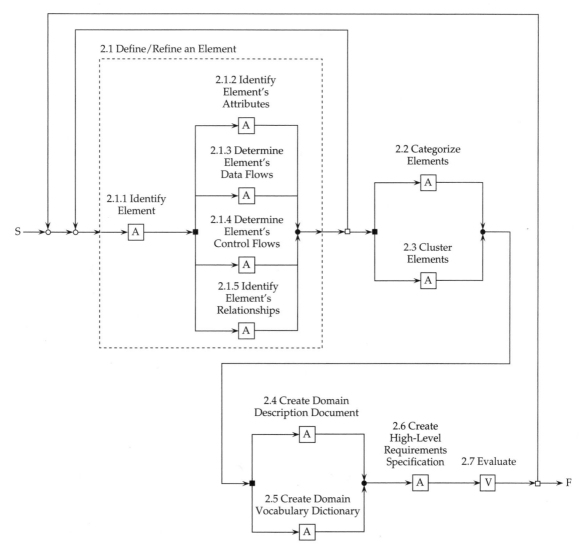

Figure A.3: Stage 2: Define/Refine Domain-Specific Elements

1. How does data flow between elements in the domain?

2. How does control flow between elements in the domain?

Stage 2.1.1: Identify a Domain Element

The basic elements in the domain should be identified and classified by describing their functional behavior, temporal/operational relationships (control flow or state transitions), or data values. This is the highest level of component identification and interface design. A more detailed and rigorous definition will take place in subsequent stages (see Stage 4.2, *Define Modules*).

1. What are the elements in the domain?

2. Is this a data or functional element?

3. What are the inputs to a (functional) element?

4. What are the outputs from a (functional) element?

5. What services/operations does this element provide?

Stage 2.1.2: Identify Attributes of Elements

Critical to the robustness of the DSSA being developed is the domain engineer's ability to address variations in "requirements" in a variety of manners. The goal of this stage in the domain engineering process, as detailed in the substages that follow, is to characterize the *required/essential* features or elements in the domain along with the *optional* features or elements. Furthermore *alternative* features or elements should be identified and trade-offs recognized and recorded where possible.

Stage 2.1.2.1: Identify Required, Essential, and Mandatory Elements. This stage in the domain engineering process tries to identify the features, elements, or concepts that are being manipulated in a domain that readily distinguishes applications in this problem domain from applications in other problem domains.

1. What are the *required/essential* elements in this problem domain?

Stage 2.1.2.2: Identify Optional Elements. The goal of this stage in the domain engineering process is to "identify differences" or things that might change from application to application within this problem domain.

1. What are the *optional* elements in this problem domain?

2. What are the reasons that these elements are optional?

Stage 2.1.2.3: Identify Alternative Elements. It has long been recognized that families of implementations [Par72] exist that provide the same functionality with different performance and space characteristics. The implementation trade-offs are addressed in later stages, but the alternative relationship between features, entities, or concepts is important to identify at this abstract level.

1. What are the *alternative* elements in this problem domain?

2. What element is this element an alternative to?

3. Is this element mutually exclusive with other elements?

4. What are the reasons that elements are alternatives?

Stage 2.1.2.4: Identify Common Requirements.   The goal of this stage in the domain-engineering process is to "factor out commonality" across applications in this domain. The domain engineer should note the special emphasis placed on the term *requirements*. This is the *first* use of the word. It is being used to identify *functional/behavioral* requirements and *temporal/operational* requirements.

   Note (for the second time): For purposes of clarity, the reader is reminded that this process makes a special distinction between a *requirement*, which is a defining characteristic in the problem space, and an implementation or design *constraint*, which is a discriminating characteristic in the solution space.

1. What are the elements that do not change from one application to another (same functionality)?

2. What requirements are common to all applications in this domain?

Stage 2.1.2.5: Identify Variable Requirements.   The goal of this stage in the domain engineering process is to classify the functional/behavior requirements or temporal/operational requirements that differentiate various applications in the domain.

1. What are the elements that change from one application to another?

2. What is the range of variation between different implementations of this element?

3. What trade-offs exist and why?

4. What alternative approaches exist and why were they not chosen?

5. What other issues may come to bear on future systems and how?

Stage 2.1.3: Determine Element's Data Flows

1. How does control flow between entities/elements in the domain?

Stage 2.1.4: Determine Element's Control Flows

1. How does control flow between entities/elements in the domain?

Stage 2.1.5: Identify Relationship Between Elements

The only relationships between elements or entities in the domain explicitly identified so far in the domain engineering process have been:

1. optional entities,

2. alternative entities,

3. required entities,

4. common entities, and perhaps

5. mutually exclusive entities.

In addition, implicit relationships have been expressed through the creation of the data-flow and control-flow (or state-transition) diagrams. The goal of this stage in the domain engineering process is to apply object-oriented analysis techniques to describe the relationships between elements previously identified in this process.

A second kind of relationship may be identifiable at this time, although it is more likely to be determined in later stages (e.g., Stage 4, *Develop Domain Architectures/Models*, or Stage 5, *Produce/Gather Reusable Work Products*). These "uses/needs" relationships may be derived from the data-flow and control-flow diagrams.

Stage 2.1.5.1: Identify "is a/kind of" Relationships. Relationships of this sort assist in building a thesaurus (see Stage 2.5.1). This relationship is the specialization/generalization relationship usually associated with inheritance in an object-oriented paradigm.

1. Is an element an instance of another element?

Stage 2.1.5.2: Identify "consists of" Relationships. This is the "aggregation" relationship associated with an object-oriented paradigm.

1. Is an element part of another element?

Stage 2.1.5.3: Identify "uses/needs" Relationships. One should examine the data-flow and control-flow diagrams for insight into identifying these relationships.

1. What elements does this element need services from?

2. What elements does this element provide services to?

Stage 2.2: Classify Elements

This step in the domain engineering process is both a classification of previously identified concepts, objects, or entities and the creation of new entities that represent classes/generalizations of the objects or entities identified as being in the domain.

1. Can elements be classified into classes?

2. Can elements be abstracted?

Stage 2.3: Cluster Common Elements

The results of Stage 2.1.5.1, *Identify "is a/kind of" Relationships*, should provide useful inputs to this stage.

1. Can elements be clustered into type hierarchies?

Stage 2.4: Create a Domain Description Document

The domain engineer should consider creating an overview document describing the elements and relationships between the elements within the domain. This may be an optional stage in the domain engineering process, because there may be textbooks or other documentation that adequately describe the material, but if such a document is not available, this stage serves as an excellent vehicle for validating progress with the domain experts. As a minimum, a list of pointers to additional documentation should be created.

1. What would the user of the DSSA like to have available as reference material?

Stage 2.5: Create a Domain Vocabulary Dictionary

This dictionary could be part of the domain description document described in Stage 2.4. The purpose of creating a dictionary of domain-specific terminology is to serve as a focal point for consensus building of the DSSA.

1. What is the vocabulary/terminology used to describe elements in this domain?

Stage 2.5.1: Create a Domain Thesaurus

Create a list of synonyms for terms in the domain.

1. What alternative terminology can be used to describe elements (synonyms)?

Stage 2.6: Create a High-Level Requirements Specification Document

The final (and optional under some circumstances) developmental stage in this phase of the domain engineering process is the creation of a "generic" (reusable) Requirements Specification Document (in MIL-STD format). While this stage is tailored to meet DoD standards, a similar end user requirements "shopping list" could be created to serve as a communications vehicle as well as advertising mechanism.

1. What user requirements map into the elements that have been identified in the previous stages of this process?

Stage 2.7: Evaluate Results and Iterate if Necessary

As stated in the introductory material, the process of creating a DSSA is an iterative process. Several sessions with the domain experts and several review cycles could be required, if necessary or desirable, to complete this step in the domain-engineering process, again, depending on the domain analysis goals.

1. Can these elements identified in the domain be broken down further?

2. Do the domain experts concur with the material generated to date?

Stage 2 Inputs

1. Outputs from Stage 1

2. Selected systems

3. Selected documentation (e.g., textbooks, articles)

Stage 2 Outputs

1. Data dictionary with thesaurus (domain ontology)

2. Type/inheritance hierarchy (domain taxonomy)

3. Generic high-level block diagram/architecture

4. Data-flow and control-flow diagrams for various aspects of applications in the domain

5. Rationale and relationships between elements in the domain

Stage 2 Validation Procedure

1. Concurrence of domain experts on the completeness and accuracy of the dictionary and thesaurus

2. Concurrence of domain experts on the completeness and accuracy of the domain description document

3. Concurrence of domain experts on the completeness and accuracy of the high-level requirements specification document

4. Concurrence of domain experts on the completeness and accuracy of the data-flow and control-flow diagrams

STAGE 3: DEFINE/REFINE DOMAIN-SPECIFIC DESIGN AND IMPLEMENTATION REQUIREMENT CONSTRAINTS

As initially stated in the *Terminology and Definitions* section, and emphasized in the Stage 2.1.2.4, *Identify Common Requirements* (for the third time), these guidelines make a special distinction between the term *requirement*, which describes a defining characteristic in the problem space, and the term *constraint*, which describes a discriminating characteristic in the solution space. This distinction is partially motivated by an observation Ruben Prieto-Díaz made in describing the Establish Global Requirements stage (A5113, Stage 1.1.3) of the STARS Domain Analysis Activities [PD91b] (see the end of this appendix) relating to two kinds of requirements in an application domain:

1. *stable*: ones that do not change from application to application and

2. *variable*: ones that do/might change.

Expanding on this observation, it is the thesis of this process that it is *ALWAYS* the case that the

- "stable" requirements are the "*what*" requirements and

- "variable" requirements are the "*how*" requirements.

The following are examples of "how" and "what" requirements:

- "what it does" (functional/behavioral requirement),

- "how often" (performance requirement),

- "how fast" (performance requirement),

- "how big,"

- "how accurate,"

- "how implemented" (physical requirements as well as language),

- "how delivered,"

- "how it looks" (user interface), and

- "how it works" (operational requirements (protocols to follow) or algorithmic alternatives).

Therefore, these "variable requirements" are referred to as *constraints* to distinguish their role in the creation of a DSSA.

The series of steps found in this phase of the domain engineering process correspond to the list of "hows" just given. The goal of this stage in the domain engineering process is to characterize the discriminating features in the solution space.

Finally, not only must the constraints be identified, but their implications on design and implementation decisions[10] should be recorded as well as any discussions related to any issues that arise in dealing with them.

Figure A.4 shows the individual steps in this process stage.

Stage 3.1: Define Constraints on Architecture

This stage of the domain engineering process identifies the overall technological, hardware, software, and performance constraints on possible implementations.[11] In general, the following two questions must be addressed in various detail:

1. What are the technology dependencies on the elements identified in Stage 2?

2. What are the design implementation dependencies on the respective elements?

Note: The domain engineer should be aware of a slight shift in emphasis on the background of the domain expert in this stage of the domain engineering process. In previous stages, the domain expertise was concentrated on the systems/requirements analysts or system engineer. In the stages to come, the software engineer plays an increasingly important role.

Stage 3.1.1: Define Software Constraints

1. What language or languages are implementations to be written in?

2. What operating system or run-time system must the software components interface with?

---

[10] Addressing design and implementation constraints relate to establishing *context* in the 3-C model.

[11] *Note*: Nontechnical constraints such as documentation and testing standards can also be addressed at this time.

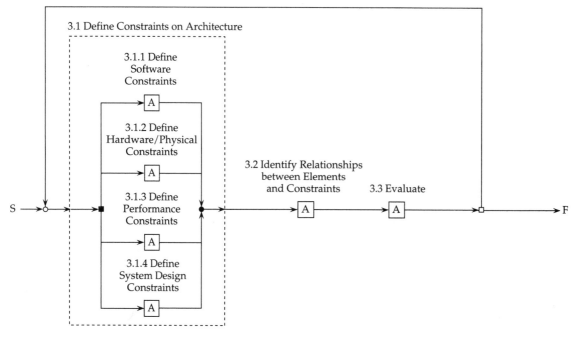

Figure A.4: Stage 3: Define/Refine Domain-Specific Design and Implementation Requirement Constraints

3. What databases is the software to run off of?

4. What communication protocols is the software to follow?

5. What external software interfaces or software development standards must the software being developed comply with?

6. What documentation does the system customer typically require?

7. How are the semantics of modules to be specified (e.g., text or formal specification language)?

Stage 3.1.2: Define Hardware/Physical Constraints

1. What platforms are the applications in this domain likely to run on?

2. What does the user interface look like?

3. What hardware is the user likely to want applications in this domain to interface with?

4. What space constraints exist on the individual elements that make up the applications in this domain?

5. What space constraints exist on the applications in this domain?

Stage 3.1.3: Define Performance Constraints

1. What timing constraints exist on the individual elements that make up applications in this domain?

2. What timing constraints exist on applications in this domain?

Stage 3.1.4: Define System Design Constraints

1. What safety, fault tolerance, or other overall design constraints could be applicable to applications in this domain?

Stage 3.2: Identify Relationships Between Elements and Constraints

The goal of this stage in the domain engineering process is to map the general design and implementation constraints identified in Stage 3.1 onto the domain-specific requirements and elements that were identified in Stage 2, *Define/Scope Domain-Specific Elements*.

If possible, issues, trade-offs, and rationale should be recorded related to how the constraints affect the subsequent design and implementations of the DSSA under development.

1. What elements identified in Stage 2 are affected by the constraints identified in the previous stages of this phase of the domain engineering process?

2. How are these elements affected and what are the design and implementation trade-offs that need to be considered?

Stage 3.3: Evaluate Results and Iterate if Necessary

Again, based on the goals of the domain engineering process, this stage may be iterated until the desired level of detail in each requirement and element is achieved.

Stage 3 Inputs

1. Outputs from Stage 1, especially the block diagram

2. Outputs from Stage 2, especially the architecture, control, and data-flow diagrams, and rationale

Stage 3 Outputs

1. List of constraints on the hardware used by applications in the domain

2. List of constraints on the software used by applications in the domain

3. List of constraints on the software developed as part of applications in the domain

4. List of performance constraints on applications in the domain

5. List of design constraints on applications in the domain

6. List of implementation constraints on applications in the domain

7. A cross-reference of constraints to the functional units/elements in the domain

Stage 3 Validation Procedure

Note: Design *and* implementation constraints are both addressed in this section. The domain engineer may find that a system analyst is better able to comment on high-level design constraints, whereas an experienced software engineer may be best suited to evaluate the low-level design and implementation constraints. Validation then becomes one of establishing:

1. Concurrence of domain experts (system analysts and software engineers) on the completeness and accuracy of the constraints identified

2. Concurrence of potential customers or marketing personnel on the completeness and accuracy of the constraints identified

STAGE 4: DEVELOP DOMAIN ARCHITECTURES/MODELS

The first three stages in this domain engineering process have focused on domain analysis—explicitly capturing domain-specific knowledge that oftentimes is implicitly assumed as common knowledge by a domain expert. The last two stages deal with the design and analysis of a DSSA and its realization through the population of the solution space with implementations (reusable software components). The unit of abstraction that is being manipulated at this stage in the domain engineering process is a model or module. As in traditional top-down design, a high-level system design (or architecture) can be decomposed into subsystems (or frameworks in the object-oriented paradigm) that themselves, in turn, can be decomposed into smaller subsystems, eventually resulting in the lowest level of abstraction of the module. At each layer of decomposition, the architecture, subsystem, or module can be modeled, analyzed, and treated as a parameterized (configurable) black box.

Different architectures (high-level designs) may be required for the same application domain because of certain constraints placed on their realization (e.g., a massively parallel host environment would be associated with a different software architecture than a sequential uniprocessor host environment). Therefore, several DSSAs may have to be designed, within one application domain, to satisfy the previously identified requirements and constraints.

The goal of this stage in the domain engineering process is to come up with generic architectures and to specify the syntax and semantics of the modules or components that form them.

Figure A.5 shows the individual steps in this process stage.

Stage 4.1: Define Domain-Specific Software Architecture(s)

Stage 4.1.1: Define a Generic High-Level Design

1. What does a generic high-level design for applications in this domain look like, based on the constraints identified in the previous stage of the domain engineering process?

2. Are several architectures needed to address all the constraints identified in the previous stage of the domain engineering process?

Stage 4.1.2: Identify High-Level Components/Modules

1. What are the components that make up the high-level design(s)/architecture(s)?

Stage 4.1.3: Define a Decision Taxonomy for Requirements and Constraints

Based on the alternatives, options, and constraints identified in the previous stages of this domain engineering process, the domain engineer should construct

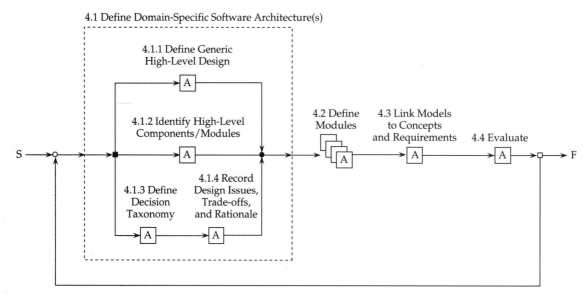

Figure A.5: Stage 4: Develop Domain Architects/Models

a series of questions to allow the end user to configure the architecture to meet the requirements and constraints applicable to a particular context.

Note: This decision taxonomy can be expressed in terms of "rules" in the form associated with expert system knowledge representation.

1. What is the first option that the end user should decide a value for?

2. What are the possible values to choose from?

3. How does the selection of certain values constrain other decisions?

4. What is the default value for this decision?

5. How is the default value determined?

6. What is the next design decision to be made?

Stage 4.1.4: Record Design Issues, Trade-Offs, and Decision Rationale

The information recorded in this stage of the domain engineering process should be a collection of the information gathered in previous stages in the process.

1. Under what circumstances are certain choices better than other choices?

2. What alternatives exist if a given choice is not available?

Stage 4.2: Define Modules

Stage 4.2.1: Specify Interfaces for Each Module

1. What are the operations associated with this module?

2. What are the data types associated with the operations in this module?

3. What are the errors or exceptions associated with this module?

4. What are the constants associated with this module?

5. What are the data objects associated with this module?

6. What issues, decisions, rationale, etc., are associated with this module?

Stage 4.2.2: Specify Semantics of Each Module

1. What is the functional behavior of this module?

2. What are the entry and exit criteria for this module?

3. What is the error or exception handling behavior of this module?

Stage 4.2.3: Specify Constraints on Each Module

Based on information gathered in previous stages of the domain engineering process, one can recognize that the solution space for each module is constrained by the various types of conditions. The goal of this stage is to associate those constraints with individual modules.

Stage 4.2.3.1: Specify Performance/Timing Constraints 1. What performance or timing constraints apply to this module?

Stage 4.2.3.2: Specify Dependency Constraints 1. What modules/data need to be imported by this module?

Stage 4.2.3.3: Specify Sequentiality/Order Constraints 1. What is the calling or timing sequence of operations within this module? 2. What is the calling or timing sequence of operations in this module with other modules?

Stage 4.2.3.4: Specify Design Constraints 1. What design constraints are associated with this module? 2. What implementation standards need to be followed?

Stage 4.2.4: Specify Performance Characteristics of Each Module

The following information may be characteristic of the algorithm selected. Because many algorithms may exist that provide the same semantic behavior, a family of modules may exist that can be differentiated by this characteristic.

1. How much time do the operations in this module take to execute, based on certain data values?

Stage 4.2.5: Identify Configuration (Generic) Parameters for Each Module

When creating a DSSA, a single-point solution is not desirable. The goal of this process is to create multiple-point solutions to increase opportunities for reuse in different contexts through adaptation and configuration parameters.

1. Based on the decision taxonomy in Stage 4.1.3 and the relationships identified in Stage 2.1.5, *Identify Relationships Between Elements*, how can this module be parameterized to increase its domain of applicability within the constraints of this application domain?

2. Can the module interfaces be designed with special "hooks" to allow for future adaptability?

Stage 4.2.6: Record Issues, Trade-Offs, and Design Rationale

Depending on the domain analysis goals, several models of the domain or portions of the domain may be created as part of a study to determine optimal configurations or algorithms based on certain assumptions, requirements, or constraints. The models, as well as the results or insights gained from using these models or simulations, should be incorporated into the knowledge base that is associated with the DSSA environment.

1. What issues were raised during interface design?

2. What alternative approaches could have been taken and why?

3. Why were things done the way they were done?

Stage 4.3: Link Modules/Models to Elements and Requirements

The goal of this stage in the domain engineering process is to create a requirements cross-reference matrix showing what modules satisfy what requirements and what portions of the problem space have been modeled.

1. How do the modules relate to the elements defined in Stage 2?

2. Which modules satisfy what requirements according to what constraints?

3. Are all requirements satisfied?

4. Do all modules satisfy at least one requirement?

5. What portions of the domain have been modeled for what purposes?

Stage 4.4: Evaluate Results and Iterate if Necessary

Again, based on the goals of the domain engineering process, this stage may be iterated until the desired level of detail in each model/module is achieved.

1. What subsystems can be further refined?

2. What additional analysis needs to be performed or recorded on the modules/models or architectures that currently define the DSSA?

Stage 4 Inputs

The inputs to this stage consist of the inputs and outputs of the previous stages.

Stage 4 Outputs

1. DSSAs

2. Domain-specific models and analysis results

3. Mappings between models/modules/subsystems and requirements identified in Stage 2

4. Mappings between models/modules/subsystems and elements identified in Stage 2

5. Mappings between models/modules/subsystems and terms that appear in the Dictionary defined in Stage 2

Stage 4 Validation Procedure

1. Concurrence of domain experts (system analysts) on the completeness and accuracy of the models defined

2. Concurrence of domain experts (software engineers) on the completeness and accuracy of the interfaces to the modules described

3. Concurrence of domain experts on the issues raised and rationale identified

STAGE 5: PRODUCE/GATHER REUSABLE WORK PRODUCTS

The last stage in this domain engineering process focuses on populating the DSSA(s) [high-level design(s)] with components that may be used to generate new applications in the problem domain. If the goal of the domain analysis was to build up a knowledge base in support of an existing application, then clearly, this step is not needed. Because, in essence, this is a software development effort, the domain experts who should be involved in this stage of the process are the software engineers who previously have created applications in this domain. They are best suited for identifying existing reusable components or components that can serve as a basis for creating reusable components. Another option is to import reusable components from some other domain. This is possible, especially in the case of low-level data structures [Boo87], utilities, and user interface software.

Figure A.6 shows the individual steps in this process stage.

Stage 5.1: Develop/Collect the Reusable Artifacts

The issue being addressed at this stage in the domain engineering process is how to determine the best source of components to populate the DSSAs. The options are to "make, buy, or modify" components that satisfy the syntax and semantics of the interfaces defined in Stage 4.2. Depending on the level of refinement performed in Stage 4 and the availability of commercial off-the-

5.1 Develop/Collect the Reusable Artifacts

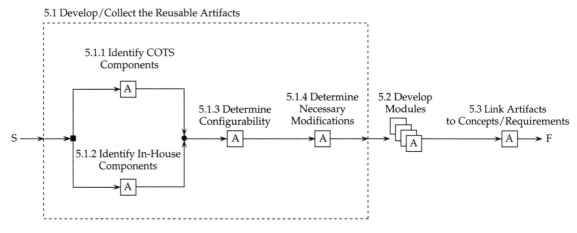

Figure A.6: Stage 5: Produce/Gather Reusable Work Products

shelf software or legacy code, interfaces may have to be modified or the specifications modified to account for differences.

Stage 5.1.1: Identify COTS Components

1. What commercially available off-the-shelf software components are available that meet the module interface specifications defined in Stage 4.2?

Stage 5.1.2: Identify In-House Components

1. What existing in-house software components are available that meet the module interface specifications defined in Stage 4.2?

Stage 5.1.3: Determine Parameterization/Configurability Level

1. What parameters make sense to have associated with certain modules based on the constraints identified in Stage 2, *Define/Scope Domain-Specific Elements*?

Stage 5.1.4: Determine Necessary Modifications

1. Do the candidate modules need to be modified? If so how much will it cost to do so? What are the impacts of changing the specification defined in Stage 4.2 instead?

2. How do the constraints identified in Stage 3 affect the design and implementation of software components for the required modules?

Stage 5.2: Develop Each Module

Stage 5.2.1: Implement Each Module

1. What language or languages should the module be implemented in?

Stage 5.2.2: Test Each Module

1. What test criteria exist for placing components into the DSSA environment?

Stage 5.2.3: Document Each Module

1. What documentation criteria (e.g., on-line, MIL-STD, etc.) need to be developed and incorporated in the DSSA environment?

Stage 5.2.4: Record Issues, Trade-Offs, and Design Rationale

This stage, as with stages of similar intent in other phases of the domain engineering process, poses the proverbial questions "Why were things done they way they were done?" and "Could they have been done differently?"

1. What trade-offs were made in determining the implementations for the components?

2. What trade-offs were made in speed and complexity for adaptability and configurability?

Stage 5.3: Link Artifacts to Models, Elements, and Requirements

The domain engineer should create several cross-reference matrices correlating the reusable software components that were implemented in this stage of the domain engineering process with previous domain-specific resources (e.g., concepts, requirements, constraints, and models/modules defined in the previous stages of the process).

Note: It is important to point out that the software work products created or gathered as part of this stage in the domain engineering process do not always correspond one-to-one with the modules decomposed in Stage 4,

Develop Domain Architectures/Models. For reasons of efficiency, or ease of implementation, module boundaries may be crossed, but these circumstances should be adequately noted and justified.

1. How were the key elements identified in Stage 2 implemented?

2. How were the requirements identified in Stage 2 met?

3. How were the requirements identified in Stage 2 tested?

4. How were the constraints identified in Stage 3 satisfied?

5. How were the semantics of the modules defined in Stage 4 tested?

Stage 5 Inputs

The work efforts for this stage of the domain engineering process use the interface specifications generated in Stage 4 and related artifacts from existing systems identified in Stage 1.

Stage 5 Outputs

1. Reusable components and associated test cases and documentation

2. Cross-reference matrices of components to requirements, constraints, and architecture

Stage 5 Validation Procedure

"The proof is in the eating of the pudding."

1. Consensus of software engineers on documentation, parameterization levels, and implementation correctness

2. Prove that new applications can be readily generated using the architecture and components

CONCLUDING REMARKS

This appendix has presented a process for creating a DSSA. Based on experience, this process should be viewed as serving as a guideline that must be tailored to fit the characteristics and resources available in each domain being analyzed. The ambitious nature of this process (i.e., long and detailed) reflects the desire for thoroughness as a trade-off for timeliness. Therefore, when applying any domain analysis process, the user must evaluate the potential return on investment for such activities and prioritize the level of detail and effort applied to meet their goals.

OVERVIEW OF STARS DOMAIN ANALYSIS ACTIVITIES

The four high-level stages in the STARS Domain Analysis Process [PD91b] are as follows.

1. *Prepare domain information*: define domain; do high-level functional analysis (top-down).

2. *Classify domain entities*: identify and describe objects and operations (bottom-up) and construct thesauri.

3. *Derive domain models*: consolidate top-down and bottom-up views to create a generic functional model based on reusable components.

4. *Expand models and classification*: apply and validate the models.

Each stage in this process is described graphically using the Structured Analysis and Design Technique [MM88] using SADT diagrams, which indicate the

- inputs,

- outputs,

- controlling factors, and

- mechanism—"agents that enable, conduct, perform or execute the activity." [PD91b]

In addition, each stage contains a textual description that provides the rationale and goals as well as directions for completing the respective activity.

The complete domain analysis process is outlined next.

Stage 1: Prepare Domain Information

Stage 1.1: Define domain

Stage 1.1.1: Select relevant information

Stage 1.1.2: Bound domain

Stage 1.1.3: Establish global requirements

Stage 1.1.4: Verify and validate definition

Stage 1.2: Obtain domain knowledge

Stage 1.2.1: Select sources of information

Stage 1.2.2: Extract domain knowledge

Stage 1.2.2.1: Read

Stage 1.2.2.2: Consult

Stage 1.2.2.3: Study

Stage 1.2.2.4: Learn

Stage 1.2.3: Review acquired domain information

Stage 1.2.3.1: Discuss

Stage 1.2.3.2: Evaluate

Stage 1.2.3.3: Integrate

Stage 1.2.3.4: Consolidate

Stage 1.3: Do high-level functional analysis (top-down)

Stage 1.3.1: Identify major functional units

Stage 1.3.2: Find interrelationships

Stage 1.3.3: Specify generic subsystems

Stage 1.3.4: Classify subsystems

Stage 1.3.4.1: Analyze common features

Stage 1.3.4.2: Group and classify

Stage 1.3.5: Select graphic representation method

Stage 2: Classify Domain Entities (bottom-up)

Stage 2.1: Identify objects and operations

Stage 2.1.1: Analyze elements

Stage 2.1.2: Analyze requirements

Stage 2.1.3: Extract component descriptors

Stage 2.1.4: Inspect documentation

Stage 2.1.5: Decompose statements by keywords

Stage 2.2: Abstract and classify

Stage 2.2.1: Group terms

Stage 2.2.2: Give names to clusters

Stage 2.2.3: Arrange by facets

Stage 2.2.4: Arrange by hierarchy

Stage 2.2.5: Define standard classification templates

    Stage 2.2.5.1: Consult STARS standards

    Stage 2.2.5.2: Check conflicts/duplication with other libraries

Stage 2.3: Expand basic classification

Stage 2.3.1: Refine meanings

Stage 2.3.2: Integrate new classes and terms

Stage 2.3.3: Group unclassified terms

Stage 2.3.4: Give names to new clusters

Stage 2.3.5: Define new templates

Stage 2.4: Construct thesauri

Stage 2.4.1: Find internal synonyms

Stage 2.4.2: Add external synonyms

Stage 2.4.3: Form thesaurus entries

Stage 2.4.4: Verify entries

Stage 3: Derive Domain Models (consolidate top-down and bottom-up)

Stage 3.1: Group descriptors/classes under functional units

Stage 3.2: Review domain models (refine initial functional decomposition)

Stage 3.3: Discover/define new functional units

Stage 3.4: Rearrange structure (result: generic functional model)

Stage 3.5: Select model representations

Stage 4: Expand Models and Classification

Stage 4.1: Apply models to application

Stage 4.2: Identify inconsistencies

Stage 4.3: Update models and classification

Stage 4.4: Define reusable structures

List of Acronyms

ADA	American Dental Association[1]
ADAGE	Avionics Domain Application Generation Environment
AI	Artificial Intelligence
ARPA	Advanced Research Projects Agency
CASE	Computer-Aided Software Engineering
CISC	Complex Instruction Set Computer
CMU	Carnegie Mellon University
COTS	Commercial Off-The-Shelf Software
DA	Domain Analysis
DARPA	Defense Advanced Research Projects Agency
DISA CIM	Defense Information Systems Agency Corporate Information Management
DoD	Department of Defense
DOMAIN	Domain Models, All INtegrated
DSSA	Domain-Specific Software Architecture
EDP	Electronic Data Processing
FODA	Feature-Oriented Domain Analysis
gIBIS	Graphical Issue-Based Information System
IC	Integrated Circuit
IDA	Institute for Defense Analysis
IPL	Initial Program Load or Intellectual Property Law
JCL	Job Control Language
KSLOC	Thousand Source Lines Of Code
KWIC	Key Word In Context

---

[1] *Not* to be confused with the programming language Ada.

MCC	Microelectronic Computer Consortium
MIL-STD	Military Standard
MIPS	Million Instructions Per Second
NIH	Not Invented Here or National Institutes of Health
NIST	National Institute of Standards and Technology
OCU	Object Connection Update Model
PM	Person-Month
POB	Persistent Object Base
POL	Problem-Oriented Language
PRL	Program Reuse Lead
PSW	Program Status Word
RDD-100	Requirements Driven Design
RIG	Reuse Interoperability Group
RISC	Reduced Instruction Set Computer
ROI	Return On Investment
ROTS	Research Off-The-Shelf Software
SEI	Software Engineering Institute
SIGADA	Special Interest Group in Ada
SIGSOFT	Special Interest Group in Software Engineering
SISTO	Systems and Information Technology Office
SLOC	Source Lines Of Code
SPC	Software Productivity Consortium
SRS	System Requirements Specification
STARS	Software Technology for Adaptable, Reliable Systems
URL	Uniform Reference Locator
VHLL	Very High Level Language
WIFM	What's In it For Me?
WIMP	Well-Intentioned but Mediocre People
WISR	Workshop on Institutionalizing Software Reuse

Glossary

Note: The glossary entries marked with an asterisk have been reused (or adapted) with permission from the *Object World Reuse Tutorial Appendix* by Eric Aranow, Martin Griss, and Marty Wosser.

Abstract Base Class An approach to organizing C++ inheritance class hierarchies such that generic interfaces and behavior are defined in a single base class and all specific implementations inherit from that.*

Application Architecture The architecture for a single system (the result of instantiating or refining a reference architecture).

Application Engineering The process of instantiating, refining, and/or extending a reference architecture.

Architecture The set of design principles, constraints, major functional components, and control/data flows that guide the developers of a system.*

Artifact Specific life cycle work products such as documents, code, tests, dictionaries, and diagrams.*

Asset A valuable and potentially reusable work product or knowledge.*

Black Box Reuse Reuse of a component without modification to its implementation. Black box components may be certified.*

Carry-Over Code Code written for a previous version of an application that is kept (reused), unmodified in the next version.

Catalog A part of a reuse library system that supports the search and selection process. The catalog often contains a name, title, abstract, keywords, and other classification information.*

Class The fundamental unit of encapsulation of objects. A class defines the attributes (data) and methods (procedures) exported by an object. These interface elements may be defined explicitly or inherited.*

Class Hierarchy A tree structure representing the inheritance or subtyping relationships among a set of classes.*

Classification The part of a reuse library (or library process) dealing with indexes, facets, keywords, and hierarchical relationship structures aimed at making it easy (or easier) to find a needed work product and sometimes to help understand the relationship of the work product to other work products.*

Cloning Taking code from one application and making modifications to it for use in another application. Similar to Software Salvaging, but functionality remains the same.

Cohesion A property of a component that measures the degree to which all references to other functional units and data lie within itself. This measures the degree of independence from other components in the library.*

Component An architectural "element" or design "module" having an interface.[1]

Coupling A property of a component that measures how much a component depends on other components.*

Data Encapsulation An interface design technique in which data are packaged with the corresponding operations on it. Furthermore, access to the data is usually restricted to only those operations.

Deposition Ratio The percentage of code that is part of a delivered application that has been put into a reuse library (explicitly made reusable).

Domain The functional area covered by a family of systems where similar software requirements exist.

Domain Analysis A study that identifies the similarities and differences among related systems within a domain.

Domain Engineering The process of creating a DSSA (domain analysis and domain modeling followed by creating a software architecture and populating it with components).

---

[1]Some confusion has always surrounded trying to define what a "component" is (e.g., an object, an abstract data type, an Ada package, an entity, etc.) because components in a domain model can be at a different level of abstraction than components in a software architecture. This has resulted in a "you'll-know-it-when-you-see-it" kind of definition.

Domain Model Any representation of elements in a domain that shows some relationship between them. In DSSA this usually consists of a lexicon, ontology, and taxonomy of the terms that characterize the domain, including objects, relationships, products, and perhaps behavioral terms such as actions and events.

DSSA (Domain-Specific Software Architecture) A software architecture with reference requirements and domain model, infrastructure to support it, and process to instantiate/refine it.

Frame A design technique for parameterizing reusable software components that allows configurability by "plugging in" code segments or parameter values.

Framework A design skeleton for an application that provides a shell for the systematic development and interconnection of components. The infrastructure that implements a system architecture.* (See DSSA)

Horizontal Domain Analysis The process of identifying functional commonality across application domains.

Information Hiding A design technique of making the implementation details of a component inaccessible to other modules.* (See Data Encapsulation)

Inheritance A language mechanism to allow the sharing of interfaces and implementations in a transitive (parent/child) manner.

Instance A concrete object, usually of some class.* The result of instantiating an Ada generic.

Instantiation The process of substituting values for parameters in macros, code templates, Ada generic packages, or other parameterized modules.

Kit A domain-oriented set of parts: a library of components, a framework for integrating them, a glue or interconnection language, a set of constraints, and a set of tools (e.g., environment, builder, etc.) to put it together [BGW92].*

Library A set of reusable assets or work products, usually well indexed, with additional classification and cataloging information to support library management.*

Megaprogramming Putting software together one component at a time, rather than one line of code at a time [Boe90].

NIH (Not Invented Here) An excuse to distrust software written by another programmer.

Overloading A language feature that allows the reuse of the name of a function or procedure in such a way that the compiler can deduce what implementation to call based on the type of data being passed.

Pattern A scheme for describing design fragments or collections of class templates such that they can be configured and reused.

Polymorphism A programming language feature that provides the ability to, at run time, direct a call to a function based on the type of data being processed. This implies several implementations of the same function with the same interface, but targeted toward different data types. (See Overloading)

PRL (Program Reuse Lead) An individual on a project who is assigned the responsibility for setting up and supervising reuse standards, processes, and education for members of a software project.

Reference Architecture A software architecture for a family of application systems.

Reference Requirements The behavioral requirements for applications in a domain.

Repository A managed library for storing and retrieving reusable work products.* (See Library)

Reusability A property or attribute that supports reuse.

Reusable Component A representation of some aspect of a system that may be used in different applications.

Reusable Software Software that was designed to be reused.

Reuse Further or repeated use.

Reuse Ratio The portion of the software on a given application that came from a reuse library.

Reuse Utility Factor A formula that takes into account the size and number of uses of a component. The rationale for this metric is that there are two factors in determining a reusable component's value: how many times it is reused and how much code didn't have to be written. The bigger the utility, the more savings achieved.

Software Architecture A collection of components, connections, and constraints/rationale that describe the design of an application.

Software-IC A term introduced by Brad Cox [Cox86] to describe software components based on a hardware analogy.*

Software Reusability The degree to which software can be reused for different applications.

Software Reuse The process of incorporating into an application software components that were designed to be reused.

Software Salvaging Taking code from one application and inserting it, with possible modifications, into a new application. Also know as **ad hoc** or **unplanned** reuse. (See Cloning)

Template A mechanism for parameterizing reusable work products. Classes are viewed as templates for objects. In C++, a template is a type-parameterized class definition, which when instantiated at compile time produces a class definition.*

Three C Model A paradigm for designing reusable software components that focuses on separating concept from content and context [Tra90b].

Toolkit A collection of high-level tools that allow the user to interact with an application framework to configure it to create a new application.

Usability Having utility.

Use The act of employing something.

Vertical Domain Analysis The process of identifying functional commonality within an application domain, for a family of applications within that domain.

White Box Reuse Reuse of work products in which access and modification of the implementation are permitted.* (See Cloning)

Bibliography

[Ada83] U.S. Department of Defense, U.S. Government Printing Office. *The Ada Programming Language Reference Manual*, 1983. ANSI/MIL-STD-1815A-1983 Document.

[Ada89] U.S. Department of Defense. Ada 9X Reference Manual. Technical Report IR-MA-1363-4, Ada 9X Mapping/Revision Team, Intermetrics, Cambridge, MA, June 1994.

[AF93] R. S. Arnold and W. B. Frakes. Software Reuse and Reengineering. In R. S. Arnold, editor, *Software Reengineering*, pages 476–484. IEEE Computer Society Press, Los Alamitos, CA, 1993.

[Ale86] N. A. Alexandridis. Adaptable Software and Hardware: Problems and Solutions. *Computer*, 19(2):29–39, February 1986.

[Ara89] G. Arango. Domain Analysis: From Art to Engineering Discipline. In *Proceedings Fifth International Workshop on Software Specification and Design*, pages 152–159, IEEE Computer Society Press, Los Alamitos, CA, May 19–20, 1989.

[Asc91] Ascent Logic Corporation. RDD-100 Requirements Driven Design User's Guide. Technical Report Release 3.0, Ascent Logic Corporation, San Jose, CA, August 1991.

[ASP93] G. Arango, E. Schoen, and R. Pettengil. Design as Evolution and Reuse. In *Proceedings of Second International Workshop on Software Reuse*, pages 9–17, March 1993.

[Bai88] S. C. Bailin. An Environment for Reusing Software Life-Cycle Products. In *Proceedings, National Conference on Software Reuseability*, Washington, D.C., April 13–14, 1988. National Institute of Software Quality and Productivity.

[Bas87] P. G. Bassett. Frame-Based Software Engineering. *IEEE Software*, 4(4):9–16, July 1987.

[BB85] B. A. Burton and M. D. Broido. A Phased Approach to Ada Package Reuse. In *Proceedings of Software Technology for Adaptable Reliable Systems (STARS) Workshop*, pages 83–98, Washington, D.C., April 9–12, 1985. STARS Program Office.

[Ber86] E. V. Berard. Creating Reusable Ada Software. In *Proceedings of National Conference on Software Reuseability and Maintainability*, Washington, D.C., September 10–11, 1986. National Institute of Software Quality and Productivity.

[BG90] A. Bunts and V. Gundrum. Lessons Learned from the Reusable Avionics Software Project (RASP). January 1990.

[BGE85] C. L. Braun, J. B. Goodenough, and R. S. Eanes. Ada Reusability Guidelines. Technical Report 3285-2-208/2, SofTech, Inc., Waltham, MA, April 1985.

[BGW92] B. W. Beach, M. L. Griss, and K. D. Wentzel. Bus-based Kits for Reusable Software. In *Proceedings of ISS'92*, pages 19–28, University of California, Irvine, Irvine, CA, March 1992.

[BHR+92] C. Braun, W. Hatch, T. Ruegsegger, B. Balzer, M. Feather, N. Goldman, and D. Wile. Domain-Specific Software Architectures—Command and Control. In *Proceedings of DARPA Software Technology Conference*, pages 215–222, Meridian Corporation, Arlington, VA, April 28–30, 1992.

[Big86a] T. J. Biggerstaff. Research Problems in Automating the Reuse of Designs. Technical Report STP-197-86, Microelectronics and Computer Technology Corporation, June 1986.

[Big86b] T. J. Biggerstaff. Reusability Overview. Technical Report STP-168-86, Microelectronics and Computer Technology Corporation, May 1986.

[Big87] T. J. Biggerstaff. Hypermedia as a Tool to Aid Large Scale Reuse. Technical Report STP-202-87, Microelectronics and Computer Technology Corporation, July 1987.

[Big91] T. J. Biggerstaff. Software Reuse Promise: Hyperbole and Reality. In *Proceedings of 13th Annual International Conference on Software Engineering*, pages 52–54, IEEE Computer Society Press, Los Alamitos, CA, May 13–17, 1991.

[BL89] P. T. Breuer and K. Lano. REDO at Oxford. In *Proceedings of the Software Re-use Workshop*, pages 39–49. Springer-Verlag, November 1989.

[BO91] D. S. Batory and S. W. O'Malley. The Design and Implementation of Hierarchical Software Systems. Technical Report TR-91-22, University of Texas, 1991.

[Boe81] B. W. Boehm. *Software Engineering Economics*. Prentice Hall, Englewood Cliffs, NJ, 1981.

[Boe90] B. W. Boehm. Domain-Specific Software Architectures and Megaprogramming. In *Proceedings of Domain-Specific Software Architecture (DSSA) Workshop*, pages 345–363, Meridian Corporation, Arlington, VA, July 11–12, 1990.

[Boo87] G. Booch. *Software Components with Ada*. Benjamin/Cummings, Menlo Park, CA, 1987.

[BP84] T. J. Biggerstaff and A. J. Perlis. Forward: Special Issue on Software Reusability. *IEEE Transactions on Software Engineering*, SE-10(5):474–476, September 1984.

[BP89] T. J. Biggerstaff and A. J. Perlis. *Software Reusability*. Addison-Wesley Publishing Company and ACM Press, New York, 1989.

[BR87a] T. Biggerstaff and C. Richter. Reusability Framework, Assessment and Directions. *IEEE Software*, 4(2):41–49, March 1987.

[BR87b] T. J. Biggerstaff and C. Richter. Reusability Framework, Assessment and Directions. In *Proceedings of the Hawaii International Conference on System Sciences*, pages 502–512, Western Periodicals Company, North Hollywood, CA, January 7–10, 1987.

[BR91] V. R. Basili and H. D. Rombach. Support for Comprehensive Reuse. Technical Report UMIACS-TR-91-23, University of Maryland, College Park, MD, February 1991.

[Bra86] U. Braun. An Expert System for the Retrieval of Software Building Blocks. Technical Report TR 05.373, IBM Laboratory, Boeblingen, West Germany, 1986. In German.

[Bro75] F. P. Brooks. *The Mythical Man-Month: Essays on Software Engineering.* Addison-Wesley Publishing Company, Reading, MA, 1975.

[Bro87] F. P. Brooks. No Silver Bullet: Essence and Accidents of Software Engineering. *IEEE Computer*, 20(4):10–19, April 1987.

[BS92] B. W. Boehm and W. L. Scherlis. Megaprogramming. In *Proceedings of Software Technology Conference 1992*, pages 63–82, Meridian Corporation, Arlington, VA, April 1992.

[Che84] T. E. Cheatham Jr. Reusability Through Program Transformations. *IEEE Transactions on Software Engineering*, SE-10(5):589–594, September 1984.

[CHSW89] J. Cramer, H. Hunnekens, W. Schafer, and S. Wolf. The MERLIN Approach to the Re-use of Software Components. In *Proceedings of the Software Re-use Workshop*, pages 57–75. Springer-Verlag, November 1989.

[CK90] M. A. Cusumano and C. F. Kemerer. A Quantitative Analysis of U.S. and Japanese Practice and Performance in Software Development. *Management Science*, 36(11):1384–1406, November 1990.

[Cox86] B. J. Cox. Object-oriented Programming, Software-ICs and System Building. In *Proceedings of National Conference on Software Reuseability and Maintainability*, Washington, D.C., September 10–11, 1986. National Institute of Software Quality and Productivity.

[Cox87] B. J. Cox. Building Malleable Systems from Software "Chips." *Computerworld*, 21(13):59–62, 64–68, March 30, 1987.

[Cox90a] B. J. Cox. Planning the Software Industrial Revolution. *IEEE Software*, 6(7):25–33, November 1990.

[Cox90b] B. J. Cox. There Is a Silver Bullet. *BYTE*, pages 209–218, October 1990.

[CP83] C. S. Chandersekaran and M. P. Perriens. Towards an Assessment of Software Reusability. In *Proceedings of ITT Workshop on Reusability in Programming*, Stratford, CT, September 7–9, 1983. ITT.

[Cro79] P. B. Crosby. *Quality Is Free: The Art of Making Quality Certain.* ITT, Stratford, CT, 1979.

[CST92] L. Coglianese, R. Smith, and W. Tracz. DSSA Case Study: Navigation, Guidance, and Flight Director Design and Development. Technical Report ADAGE-IBM-92-05, IBM Federal Systems Company, March 1992.

[Cur83] B. Curtis. Cognitive Issues in Reusability. In *Proceedings of ITT Workshop on Reusability in Programming*, Stratford, CT, September 7–9, 1983. ITT.

[Cus91] M. A. Cusumano. *Japan's Software Factories*. Oxford University Press, New York, 1991.

[Dav92] M. J. Davis. STARS Reuse Maturity Model: Guidelines for Reuse Strategy Formulation. In *Proceedings WISR'92 5th Annual Workshop on Software Reuse*, October 1992.

[Dav93] T. Davis. The Reuse Capability Model: A Basis for Improving an Organization's Reuse Capability. In *Proceedings of Second International Workshop on Software Reuse*, pages 126–133, IEEE Computer Society Press, Los Alamitos, CA, March 1993.

[Dav94] T. Davis. The Reuse Capability Model. *CrossTalk, The Journal of Defense Software Engineering*, pages 5–9, March 1994.

[Den81] P. J. Denning. Throwaway Programs. *Communications of the ACM*, 24(2):259–260, February 1981.

[Den86] R. J. St. Dennis. A Guidebook for Writing Reusable Source Code in Ada. Technical Report, Honeywell Inc., Golden Valley, MN, March 1986.

[Dij72] E. W. Dijkstra. The Humble Programmer. *Communications of the ACM*, 15(10): 859–866, October 1972.

[DRR83] L. E. Druffel, S. T. Redwine, and W. E. Riddle. The STARS Program: Overview and Rationale. *Computer*, 16(11):21–29, November 1983.

[DSFO86] R. J. St. Dennis, P. Stachour, E. Frankowski, and E. Onuegbe. Measurable Characteristics of Reusable Ada Software. *ACM SIGADA Letters*, 5(2):41–49, March/April 1986.

[DW92] T. Davis and R. Williams. Toward a Reuse Maturity Model. In *Proceedings WISR'92 5th Annual Workshop on Software Reuse*, University of Maine, Orono, ME, October 1992.

[Eam73] C. Eames and R. Eames. *A Computer Perspective*. Harvard Press, Cambridge, MA, 1973.

[FG90] W. B. Frakes and P. B. Gandel. Representing Reusable Software. *Information and Software Technology*, 32(10):653–664, December 1990.

[Fis94] D. A. Fisher. Supplemental Information for Program Competition 94-06, May 1994. Part of Advanced Technology Program—Focused Program in Component-Based Software.

[FP94] W. B. Frakes and T. P. Pole. An Empirical Study of Representation Methods for Reusable Software Components. *IEEE Transactions on Software Engineering*, 20(8):617–630, August 1994.

[Fra91] W. B. Frakes. Software Reuse: Is It Delivering? In *Proceedings of 13th Annual International Conference on Software Engineering*, page 52, IEEE Computer Society Press, Los Alamitos, CA, May 13–17, 1991.

[Fra93] W. B. Frakes. Software Reuse as Industrial Experiment. *American Programmer*, 6(5):27–33, September 1993.

[Fre83] P. Freeman. Reusable Software Engineering: Concepts and Research Directions. In *Proceedings of ITT Workshop on Reusability in Programming*, Stratford, CT, September 7–9, 1983. ITT.

[GAO93] Software Reuse—Major Issues Need to Be Resolved Before Benefits Can Be Achieved. Technical Report GAO/IMTEC-93-16, Government Accounting Office, January 1993.

[GD89] J. E. Gafney, Jr. and T. Durek. Software Reuse—Key to Enhanced Productivity: Some Quantitative Models. *Information and Software Technology*, 31(5), June 1989.

[GFP93] M. L. Griss, J. Favaro, and P. Walton. Managerial and Organizational Issues—Starting and Running a Software Reuse Program, Chapter 3. In *Software Reusability*, pages 51–78. Ellis Horwood, Chichester, UK, October 1993.

[GM92] M. Graham and E. Mettala. The Domain-Specific Software Architecture Program. In *Proceedings of DARPA Software Technology Conference, 1992*, pages 204–210, Meridian Corporation, Arlington, VA, April 1992. Also published in *CrossTalk, The Journal of Defense Software Engineering*, pages 19–21, 32, October 1992.

[GN86] P. C. Grabow and W. B. Nobles. Reusable Software Concepts and Software Development Methodologies. In *Proceedings of National Conference on Software Reuseability and Maintainability*, Washington, D.C., September 10–11, 1986. National Institute of Software Quality and Productivity.

[Gog89] J. A. Goguen. Principles of Parameterized Programming. In *Software Reusability, Volume I, Concepts and Models*, pages 159–225. Addison-Wesley Publishing Company, Reading, MA, 1989.

[GR83] A. Goldberg and D. Robson. *Smalltalk-80: The Language and Its Implementation*. Addison-Wesley Publishing Company, Reading, MA, 1983.

[Gri89] D. Gries. *The Science of Programming*. Springer-Verlag, Berlin, 1989.

[Gri91] M. L. Griss. Software Reuse at Hewlett-Packard. In *Proceedings of the First International Workshop on Software Reusability*, pages 18–24, published electronically on the Internet, July 1991.

[Gri93a] M. L. Griss. Software Reuse: From Library to Factory. *IBM Systems Journal*, 32(4):548–566, 1993.

[Gri93b] M. L. Griss. Towards Tools and Languages for Hybrid Domain-Specific Kits. In *Proceedings Sixth Annual Workshop on Software Reuse (WISR 6)*, University of Maine, Orono, ME, November 1993.

[GW94] M. L. Griss and K. D. Wentzel. Hybrid Domain-Specific Kits for a Flexible Software Factory. In *Proceedings 1994 ACM Symposium on Applied Computing (SAC'94) Software Reuse Track*, ACM, New York, March 6–8, 1994.

[HM84] E. Horowitz and J. B. Munson. An Expansive View of Reusable Software. *IEEE Transactions on Software Engineering*, SE-10(5):477–487, September 1984.

[HSH⁺86] S. Honiden, N. Sueda, A. Hoshi, N. Uchihira, and K. Mikame. Software Prototyping with Reusable Components. *Journal of Information Processing (Japan)*, 9(3): 123–129, 1986.

[HTN94] J. Higgins, W. Tracz, and E. Newton. DOMAIN (DOmain Models, All INtegrated) User Guide. Technical Report ADAGE-LOR-94-06A, Loral Federal Systems, Owego, NY, September 1994.

[Hug89] J. Hughes. Why Functional Programming Matters. *The Computer Journal*, 32(2), 1989.

[Iso92] S. Isoda. Experience Report on Software Reuse Project: Its Structure, Activities, and Statistical Results. In *Proceedings of 12th Annual International Conference on Software Engineering*, pages 320–326, May 1992.

[ITT83] *Workshop on Reusability in Programming*. Stratford, CT, 1983. ITT.

[JF88] R. E. Johnson and B. Foot. Designing Reusable Classes. *Journal of Object-Oriented Programming*, 2(1):22–35, June/July 1988.

[Jon84] T. C. Jones. Reusability in Programming: A Survey of the State of the Art. *IEEE Transactions on Software Engineering*, SE-10(5):488–493, September 1984.

[Jon86] T. C. Jones. *Programming Productivity*. McGraw-Hill Book Company, New York, 1986.

[JTPA81] R. Jefferies, A. A. Turner, P. G. Polson, and M. E. Atwood. The Processes Involved in Designing Software. In J. R. Anderson, editor, *Cognitive Skills and Their Acquisition*, Number 11, Erlbaum, Hillsdale, NJ, 1981.

[Kan86] S. Kaneko. Technology for Development and Reuse of Software Parts. *Toshiba Review*, 42(8):11–14, 1986. In Japanese.

[KCH⁺90] K. C. Kang, S. G. Cohen, J. A. Hess, W. E. Novak, and A. S. Peterson. Feature-Oriented Domain Analysis (FODA) Feasibility Study. Technical Report CMU/ SEI-90-TR-21, Software Engineering Institute, November 1990.

[KH91] P. Koltun and A. Hudson. A Reuse Maturity Model. In *Proceedings WISR'91 4th Annual Workshop on Software Reuse*, University of Maine, Orono, ME, November 1991.

[KP78] B. Kernighan and P. Plauger. *The Elements of Style*. McGraw-Hill Book Company, New York, 1978.

[KR79] W. Kunz and H. Q. J. Rittel. Issues as Elements of Information Systems. Technical Report Working Paper No. 131, Institut Fur Grundlagen Der Planung IA, University of Stuttgart, 1979.

[Lea88] K. J. Lee et al. An OOD Paradigm for Flight Simulators, 2nd Edition. Technical Report CMU/SEI-88-TR-30, Software Engineering Institute, 1988.

[LG84] R. G. Lanergan and C. A. Grasso. Software Engineering with Reusable Design and Code. *IEEE Transactions on Software Engineering*, SE-10(5):498–501, September 1984.

[LP91] P. Luckey and R. Pittman. Improving Software Quality Utilizing An Integrated CASE Environment. In *Proceedings of NAECON'91*, IEEE Service Center, Piscataway, NJ, 1991.

[LSW87] M. Lenz, H. A. Schmid, and P. F. Wolf. Software Reuse Through Building Blocks: Concepts and Experience. *IEEE Software*, 4(4):34–42, July 1987.

[Lub86] M. D. Lubars. Reusability in the Large versus Code Reusability in the Small. *ACM SIGSOFT Software Engineering Notes*, 11(1):21–27, January 1986.

[Lub87] M. D. Lubars. Schematic Techniques for High Level Support of Software Specifications. In *Proceedings of the Fourth International Workshop on Software Specification and Design*, pages 68–75, 1987. IEEE.

[Mat84] T. Matsumoto. Some Experience in Promoting Reusable Software: Presentation in Higher Abstract Levels. *IEEE Transactions on Software Engineering*, SE-10(5):502–512, September 1984.

[Mat86] Y. Matsumoto. Experiences in Software Manufacturing. In *Proceedings of National Computer Conference*, pages 93–94, 1986.

[Mat87] Y. Matsumoto. A Software Factory: An Overall Approach to Software Production. In Peter Freeman, editor, *Tutorial: Software Reusability*, pages 155–178, IEEE Computer Society Press, Los Alamitos, CA, 1987.

[Mat91] K. Matsumura. Software Reuse—What Is Different with Ordinary Software Development? In *Proceedings of 13th Annual International Conference on Software Engineering*, pages 55–57, IEEE Computer Society Press, Los Alamitos, CA, May 13–17, 1991.

[McI69] M. D. McIlroy. Mass Produced Software Components. In *Proceedings of NATO Conference on Software Engineering*, pages 88–98, Petrocelli/Charter, New York, 1969.

[McN86] D. G. McNicholl. CAMP: Common Ada Missile Packages. In *Proceedings of National Conference on Software Reuseability and Maintainability*, Washington, D.C., September 10–11, 1986. National Institute of Software Quality and Productivity.

[Met90] E. G. Mettala. Domain-Specific Software Architectures. Presentation at ISTO Software Technology Community Meeting, June 1990.

[Mey82] B. Meyer. Principles of Package Design. *Communications of the ACM*, 25(7):419–428, July 1982.

[Mey87] B. Meyer. Software Reusability: The Case for Object-Oriented Design. *IEEE Software*, 4(2):50–64, March 1987.

[MFYO87] K. Matsumura, K. Furuya, A. Yamashiro, and T. Obi. Trend Toward Reusable Module Component: Design and Coding Technique 50SM. In *Proceedings of COMPSAC 87*, IEEE Computer Society Press, Los Alamitos, CA, 1987.

[MHK⁺91] M. Matsumoto, A. Hayano, T. Kudo, H. Yoshida, S. Imai, and K. Ohshima. Specifications Reuse Process Modeling and Case Study-Based Evaluations. In *Proceedings of 15th Annual International Computer Software and Applications Conference*, pages 499–506, IEEE Computer Society Press, Los Alamitos, CA, September 1991.

[Mil56] G. A. Miller. The Magical Number Seven Plus or Minus Two: Some Limits on Our Capacity to Process Information. *Psychological Review*, 63:81–97, 1956.

[Mis87] F. C. Mish, editor. *Webster's Ninth New Collegiate Dictionary*. Merriam-Webster, New York, 1987.

[MM88] D. A. Marca and C. M. McGowan. *SADT Structured Analysis and Design Technique*. McGraw-Hill Book Company, New York, 1988.

[MMM94] A. Mili, R. Mili, and R. Mittermeir. Storing and Retrieving Software Components: A Refinement-Based System. In *Proceedings of 16th Annual International Conference on Software Engineering*, pages 91–102, IEEE Computer Society Press, Los Alamitos, CA, May 16–21, 1994.

[Mos93] L. K. Mosemann, II. Software Technology Conference Closing Address. In *Crosstalk: The Journal of Defense Software, Special Edition*, pages 2–4, 1993.

[MR83] C. McFarland and T. Rawlings. DARTS: Software Manufacturing Technology. In *Arionics Industry Aerospace Association 21st Aerospace Sciences Meeting*, page 6, January 10–13, 1983.

[MRRH81] K. B. Mckeithen, J. S. Reiman, H. H. Rueer, and S. C. Hirle. Knowledge Organization and Skill Differences in Computer Programmers. *Psychological Review*, 13:307–325, 1981.

[MSN⁺81] T. Matsubara, O. Sasaki, K. Nakajim, K. Takezawa, S. Yamamoto, and T. Tanaka. SWB System: A Software Factory. In *Software Engineering Environments*, pages 305–318, North-Holland Publishing Company, 1981.

[MT93] N. Mii and T. Takeshita. Software Re-Engineering and Reuse From a Japanese Point of View. *Information and Software Technology*, 35(1):45–53, January 1993.

[MYTT90] K. Matsumura, A. Yamashiro, T. Tanaka, and I. Takahashi. Modeling of Software Reusable Component Approach and Its Case Study. In *Proceedings of 14th Annual International Computer Software and Applications Conference*, pages 307–313, IEEE Computer Society Press, Los Alamitos, CA, October 1990.

[Onu87] E. O. Onuegbe. Software Classification as an Aid to Reuse: Initial Use as Part of a Rapid Prototyping System. In *Proceedings of the Hawaii International Conference on System Sciences*, pages 521–529, Western Periodicals Company, North Hollywood, CA, January 7–10, 1987.

[Par72] D. L. Parnas. A Technique for Software Module Specification with Examples. *Communications of the ACM*, 15(5):330–336, May 1972.

[Par76] D. L. Parnas. On the Design and Development of Software Families. *IEEE Transactions on Software Engineering*, SE-2(1):1–9, January 1976.

[PB88] C. Potts and G. Bruns. Recording Reasons for Design Decisions. In *Proceedings of Tenth International Conference on Software Engineering*, pages 418–427, IEEE Computer Society Press, Los Alamitos, CA, 1988.

[PCC91] M. Paulk, B. Curtis, and M. B. Chrissis. Capability Maturity Model for Software. Technical Report CMU/SEI-91-TR-24, Software Engineering Institute, 1991.

[PCH93] J. S. Poulin, J. M. Caruso, and D. R. Hancock. The Business Case for Software Reuse. *IBM Systems Journal*, 32(4):567–594, 1993.

[PCW83] D. L. Parnas, P. C. Clements, and D. M. Weiss. Enhancing Reusability with Information Hiding. In *Proceedings of ITT Workshop on Reusability in Programming*, Stratford, CT, September 7–9, 1983. ITT.

[PD85] R. Prieto-Díaz. *A Software Classification Scheme*. PhD thesis, University of California, Irvine, 1985.

[PD87] R. Prieto-Díaz. Domain Analysis for Reusability. In *Proceedings of COMPSAC'87*, pages 23–29, IEEE Computer Society Press, Los Alamitos, CA, 1987.

[PD91a] R. Prieto-Díaz. Reuse in the U.S. In *Proceedings of 13th Annual International Conference on Software Engineering*, pages 57–59, IEEE Computer Society Press, Los Alamitos, CA, May 13–17, 1991.

[PD91b] R. Prieto-Díaz. Reuse Library Process Model. Technical Report AD-B157091, IBM CDRL 03041-002, STARS, July 1991.

[PDA91] R. Prieto-Díaz and G. Arango. *Domain Analysis and Software Systems Modeling*. IEEE Computer Society Press, Los Alamitos, CA, 1991.

[PDF87] R. Prieto-Díaz and P. Freeman. Classifying Software for Reusability. *IEEE Software*, 4(1):6–16, January 1987.

[Pip92] J. Piper. DoD Software Reuse Vision and Strategy. *CrossTalk, The Journal of Defense Software Engineering*, (37):2–8, October 1992.

[Pol73] G. Polya. *How To Solve It*. Princeton University Press, Princeton, NJ, 1973.

[Pol86] W. Polak. Maintainability and Reusable Program Designs. In *Proceedings of National Conference on Software Reuseability and Maintainability*, Washington, D.C., September 10–11, 1986. National Institute of Software Quality and Productivity.

[Pou95] J. S. Poulin. Populating an Enterprise Wide Reusable Software Library. To appear in *Journal of Systems and Software*, 1995.

[PPA91] IBM Corporation. *Programming Process Architecture, Version 2.1*, 1991.

[Rat87] M. Ratcliffe. Report on a Workshop on Software Reuse held at Hereford, UK, on May 1–2, 1986. *SIGSOFT Software Engineering Notes*, 12(1):42–47, January 1987.

[RH83] W. B. Rauch-Hindin. Reusable Software. *Electronic Design*, 31(3):176–193, February 3, 1983.

[Sam90] P. Samuelson. Reverse-Engineering Someone Else's Software: Is It Legal? *IEEE Software*, 7(1):90-96, January 1990.

[Sam92] P. Samuelson. Updating the Copyright Look and Feel Lawsuits? *Communications of the ACM*, 35(9):25–31, September 1992.

[SE83] E. Soloway and K. Ehrlich. What Do Programmers Reuse? Theory and Experiment. *In Proceedings of ITT Workshop on Reusability in Programming*, Stratford, CT, September 7–9, 1983. ITT.

[SE84] E. Soloway and K. Ehrlich. Empirical Studies of Programming Knowledge. *IEEE Transactions on Software Engineering*, SE-10(5):595–609, September 1984.

[Sel91] R. Selby. Metric Driven Analysis and Feedback Systems for Enabling Empirically Guided Software Development. In *Proceedings of ICSE 13*, IEEE Computer Society Press, Los Alamitos, CA, May 1991.

[SMC74] W. P. Stevens, G. J. Myers, and L. L. Constantine. Structured Design. *IBM Systems Journal*, 2:115–139, 1974.

[Sol93] E. Soloway. Should We Teach Students to Program? *Communications of the ACM*, 36(10):21–24, October 1993.

[SPC93] Reuse Adoption Guidebook, Version 02.00.05. Technical Report SPC-29051-CMC, Software Productivity Consortium, Herndon, VA, 1993.

[Sta84] T. A. Standish. An Essay on Software Reuse. *IEEE Transactions on Software Engineering*, SE-10(5):494–497, September 1984.

[STA92] *STARS'92, On the Road to Megaprogramming*. Three-volume conference proceedings, STARS Technology Center, Arlington, VA, 1992.

[Str86] B. Stroustrup. *The C++ Programming Language*. Addison-Wesley Publishing Company, Reading, MA, 1986.

[TC92] W. Tracz and L. Coglianese. DSSA Engineering Process Guidelines. Technical Report ADAGE-IBM-92-02A, IBM Federal Systems Company, Owego, NY, December 1992.

[TC93a] RIG Technical Committee 2 (TC2). A Basic Interoperability Data Model for Reuse Libraries. Technical Report SDS-0001 v.2, Reuse Library Interoperability Group (RIG), February 1993.

[TC93b] W. Tracz and L. Coglianese. An Adaptable Software Architecture for Integrated Avionics. In *Proceedings of NAECON'93*, pages 1161–1168, IEEE Service Center, Piscataway, NJ, May 1993.

[TG93] J. R. Tirso and H. Gregorius. Management of Reuse at IBM. *IBM Systems Journal*, 32(4):612–615, 1993.

[TM84] D. Tajima and T. Matsubara. Inside the Japanese Software Industry. *IEEE Computer*, pages 34–43, March 1984.

[TM87] D. Tajima and T. Matsubara. The Influence of Cultural and Social Aspects on the Japanese Software Development Environment. In *Proceedings of the 1987 Fall Joint Computer Conference*, pages 246–253, Computer Society Press of IEEE, Washington, DC, October 25–29, 1987.

[TMTT92] M. Tsuda, M. Morioka, Y. Takadachi, and M. Takahashi. Productivity Analysis of Software Development with an Integrated CASE Tool. In *Proceedings of the 14th International Conference on Software Engineering*, pages 49–58, IEEE Computer Society Press, Los Alamitos, CA, May 1992.

[Tra79] W. Tracz. Computer Programming and the Human Thought Process. *Software-Practice and Experience*, 9:127–137, 1979.

[Tra82] W. Tracz. Microprogramming Glossary. *ACM SIGMicro Newsletter*, 13(2):18–23, June 1982.

[Tra86] W. Tracz. Why Reusable Software Isn't. In *Proceedings of Workshop on Future Directions in Computer Architecture and Software*, Washington, D.C., May 1986.

[Tra87a] W. Tracz. Ada Reusability Efforts—A Survey of the State of the Practice. In *Proceedings of Fifth National Conference on Ada Technology and Fourth Washington Ada Symposium*, pages 35–44, ACM, New York, March 17–19, 1987.

[Tra87b] W. Tracz. RECIPE: A Reusable Software Paradigm. In *Proceedings of the Hawaii International Conference on System Sciences*, pages 546–555, January 7–10, 1987.

[Tra87c] W. Tracz. Software Reuse: Motivators and Inhibitors. In *Proceedings of COMPCON87*, pages 358–363, IEEE Computer Society Press, Los Alamitos, CA, February 1987.

[Tra87d] W. Tracz. Software Reuse: The State of the Practice. Handouts for tutorial at COMPCON'87, February 1987.

[Tra88a] W. Tracz. RMISE Workshop on Software Reuse Meeting Summary. In *Software Reuse: Emerging Technology*, pages 41–53. IEEE Computer Society Press, Los Alamitos, CA, 1988.

[Tra88b] W. Tracz. *Software Reuse: Emerging Technology*. IEEE Computer Society Press, Los Alamitos, CA, 1988.

[Tra88c] W. Tracz. Software Reuse Maxims. *ACM Software Engineering Notes*, 13(4):28–31, October 1988.

[Tra89] W. Tracz. Parameterization: A Case Study. *ACM SIGADA Letters*, IX(4):92–102, May/June 1989.

[Tra90a] W. Tracz. Modularization: Approaches to Reuse in Ada. *Journal of Pascal, Ada & Modula-2*, 9(5):10–25, September/October 1990.

[Tra90b] W. Tracz. The 3 Cons of Software Reuse. In *Proceedings of Fourth Workshop on Software Reuse*, Syracuse University, Syracuse, NY, July 1990.

[Tra91a] W. Tracz. A Conceptual Model for Megaprogramming. *ACM Software Engineering Notes*, 16(3):36–45, July 1991.

[Tra91b] W. Tracz. Legal Obligations for Software Reuse: A Repository Scenario. *American Programmer*, 4(3):12–17, April 1991.

[Tra92] W. Tracz. Software Reuse Technical Opportunities. In *Proceedings of DARPA Software Technology Conference, 1992*, pages 33–41, Meridian Corporation, Arlington, VA, April 1992.

[Tra93a] W. Tracz. LILEANNA: A Parameterized Programming Language. In *Proceedings of Second International Workshop on Software Reuse*, pages 66–78, IEEE Computer Society Press, Los Alamitos, CA, March 1993.

[Tra93b] W. Tracz. Parameterized Programming in LILEANNA. In *Proceedings of ACM Symposium on Applied Computing SAC'93*, pages 77–86, February 1993. ACM.

[Tra93c] W. Tracz. Second International Workshop on Software Reuse Workshop Summary. *ACM Software Engineering Notes*, 18(3):A73–77, July 1993.

[Ude94] J. Udell. Component Software. *BYTE*, pages 46–55, May 1994.

[Wea86] E. Wald et al. STARS Reusability Guidebook. Draft Version 4.0, Workshop Product, September 1986.

[Weg83] P. Wegner. Varieties of Reusability. In *Proceedings of ITT Workshop on Reusability in Programming*, Stratford, CT, September 7–9, 1983. ITT.

[WES87] S. N. Woodfield, D. W. Embley, and D. T. Scott. Can Programmers Reuse Software? *IEEE Software*, 4(4):52–59, July 1987.

[Whe87] *Whelan Associates, Inc. v. Jaslow Dental Laboratories, Inc.*, 1987. 797 F.2d 1222(3d Cir. 1986), *cert. denied*, 93 L.Ed. 2d 831.

[YT92] P. S. Young and R. N. Taylor. Teamware: Process Programming Support for Managers and Teams, University of California, Irvine, technical report, July 1992.

Index

A

50 Steps per Module, 11, 132
abstract base class, 211
abstract data type, 141, 212
abstraction, 10, 95
Ada, 11, 29, 36, 69, 96, 99, 117, 140, 213
Ada 9X, 31, 117
ADAGE, 160
adaptability, 140, 176
ad hoc reuse, 107, 140
aggregation, 189
algorithm animation, 139, 145
analogical reasoning, 106
APL, 34, 70
application architecture, 211
application engineering, 211
application generator, 70, 106, 129, 140, 153, 154
application generator generator, 139, 144
archetype, 15
architecture, 168, 197, 211
ARPA, 19, 20, 41, 85, 113, 116, 120, 137, 159
artifact, 211
automatic programming, 116

B

Barnes, Bob, 53
Bell Labs, 105, 138, 156
Berard, Ed, 51, 96
Biggerstaff, Ted, xii, 12, 15, 94, 95, 137, 141, 148, 149
Biggerstaff's Reuse Rules of Three, 94
black box reuse, 29, 31, 41, 115, 128, 197, 211
Boehm, Barry, 41, 85
Booch, Grady, 2
Bryan, Doug, 31
building blocks, 97, 125, 140
business case, 16, 19, 155

C

C++, 117, 211, 215
carry-over code, 7, 73, 156, 211
CASE, 41, 74, 89, 101, 106, 113, 118, 124

catalog, 211
chunking, 129
CISC, 65, 98, 100
class, 107, 211
class hierarchy, 211
classification, 143, 148, 151, 189, 212
class library, 138
cloning, 212
clustering, 189
CMS, 102
CMU, 89
COBOL, 69, 103
code reuse, 10, 12, 13, 126, 128, 130
code review, 15
coercion, 107
Coglianese, Lou, 165
cognitive psychology, 129
Cohen, Sholom, 165
cohesion, 98, 119, 212
component, 142, 143, 168, 197, 203, 212
component-based approach, 134
component-based software industry, 5, 152
component catalog, 119
composability, 176
composition, 140
compositional optimizers, 139, 144
composition language, 139
comp.sw.components, 160
configurability, 176, 203
configuration management, 149
control flow diagram, 144, 188
copyright, 27, 82, 112
CORBA, 120
cost of reuse, 18, 47, 74, 103, 114, 115, 134, 137, 156
cost reduction, 125, 131
COTS, 112, 203
coupling, 26, 97, 119, 212
critical mass, 16, 117, 131, 134, 148, 155
Crosby, Phillip, 104
Curtis, Bill, 129

D

DARPA, 85, 168
data abstraction, 70, 106